233

Kenneth Patchen

and American Mysticism

Kenneth Patchen

and American Mysticism

by Raymond Nelson

The University of North Carolina Press

Chapel Hill and London

Manufactured in the United States of America

Library of Congress Cataloging in Publication Data

Nelson, Raymond, 1938–
   Kenneth Patchen and American mysticism.

   Bibliography: p.
   Includes index.
   1. Patchen, Kenneth, 1911–1972—Criticism and interpretation.
I. Title.
PS3531.A764Z77   1984   811'.54   83-27384
ISBN 0-8078-1610-8

A portion of this study appeared in somewhat different form in the *Rocky Mountain Review of Language and Literature* 30 (1976): 1–26.
The following publishers have granted permission for quoting selections from their works:
THE BOBBS-MERRILL COMPANY, INC.

Kenneth Patchen, "from 'A Note on *The Hunted City*,'" in *Naked Poetry*, edited by Stephen Berg and Robert Mezey, ©1969 by The Bobbs-Merrill Company, Inc.
CITY LIGHTS BOOKS

Allen Ginsberg, *Kaddish and Other Poems*, © 1961 by Allen Ginsberg
NEW DIRECTIONS PUBLISHING COMPANY

William Carlos Williams, *Collected Earlier Poems of William Carlos Williams*, ©1938 by New Directions Publishing Corporation

Kenneth Patchen, *Collected Poems of Kenneth Patchen*, © 1936, 1942, 1943, 1945, 1946, 1952, 1963, 1968 by Kenneth Patchen, © 1939, 1942, 1949, 1954, 1957, 1967 by New Directions Publishing Corporation; *Doubleheader*, © 1946, 1957, 1958 by Kenneth Patchen; *Hallelujah Anyway*, © 1960, 1966 by Kenneth Patchen; *The Journal of Albion Moonlight*, © 1941 by Kenneth Patchen; *Memoirs of a Shy Pornographer*, © 1945 by Kenneth Patchen; *Sleepers Awake*, © 1946 by Kenneth Patchen; *When We Were Here Together*, © 1952 by Kenneth Patchen, © 1957 by New Directions Publishing Corporation; *Wonderings*, © 1971 by Kenneth Patchen
UNIVERSITY OF NEBRASKA PRESS

V. K. Chari, *Whitman: In the Light of Vedantic Mysticism*, © 1964 by the University of Nebraska Press
VIKING PENGUIN INC.

John Steinbeck, *The Log from the Sea of Cortez*, © 1951 by John Steinbeck, © 1979 by Elaine Steinbeck

To the memory of

Breece D'J Pancake

*I do not say these things for a dollar or to
fill up the time while I wait for a boat*

Contents

Preface

I am jealous and overwhelm'd with friendliness,
And will go gallivant with the light and air myself.
—Whitman, "The Sleepers"

I wrote the first version of this study in the late 1960s, when
Kenneth Patchen was still alive and periodic eruptions of political
invective, a stream of fanciful poem-paintings, and an occasional
book still issued forth from his invalid's room in the modest
bungalow he had been able to buy in Palo Alto, California.
Patchen then had a remarkably bad reputation among most literary
people, and I was frequently asked why I had chosen to risk my
time and perhaps part of my own reputation on him. Because I
work among scholars, the question was usually a sympathetic
expression of intellectual curiosity. But often it was patronizing.
Sometimes it was downright hostile. One publisher's reader of my
original manuscript suggested that "Patchen's work doesn't de-
serve this kind of scrutiny, except, perhaps, as a study in the
pathology of the Whitmanian campfollower."[1]

Neither the suspicions nor the hostilities of my colleagues were
hard to understand. Patchen had seemed to dedicate himself to
antagonizing people. During the late thirties he had been greeted
almost as a young Shelley, who might discover a truly eloquent
literature in the proletarian movement, but, with the complicated
realignments of loyalties among American leftists during the years
of the Spanish Civil War, the Moscow trials, and the onset of
World War II, he set himself apart and began calling people
names. As the war progressed, he became a radical pacifist. Ev-
eryone else, he said, or almost everyone, had sold out. He accused
individuals by name, questioned their motives and integrity, and
developed an especially strident hatred of liberalism. His position

was intolerant and his language was intemperate—crude often, or shrill. For all of his life he kept up his wrathful denunciations of intellectuals, politicians, or anyone else who could find justifications for war or who used moral rhetoric in support of nationalism. "Blasphemers," he called such people, "of God & of Man! Of Life itself[.] This Treason! this Monstrous, Inhuman Betrayal! this Hideous and Cancerous Assault on all that man has been!" The passage is from a silk-screened calligraphic prophecy Patchen sent out as a Christmas message in 1970, barely more than a year before his death.[2] He paid similar attention to aesthetic critics and artists, who had also, he insisted, betrayed their communal responsibilities, and he never tired of mocking the obsession with structure and craftsmanship that characterized American writers in the decades during and after World War II. He called their work "Gold-plated poems/ to stuff up/ their mind's ass."[3] Not surprisingly, he made enemies. I have known an eminent poet literally to turn purple at the mention of Patchen's name, and his anger was the more disturbing because he was of a literary persuasion that might ordinarily have led him to ally himself with Patchen's anti-new critical position.

I have found nourishment in Patchen's work from the time when I was twenty and stumbled across it in the Gotham Book Mart. Later I lived for several years in his town, knew a number of his friends, once visited his home, and had a memorable telephone conversation with him, but he was a sick man then, and I never met him in the flesh. Even such peripheral contacts, however, were enough to confirm the sense of the troublesome personality one finds in his books. When he was not displaying his genius as one of the most talented and inventive of the second generation of American modernists he was often self-indulgent, noisy, and stubborn to a fault. William Blake's observation that "the road of excess leads to the palace of wisdom" had obviously encouraged him more than it should. Moreover, his defenders (with honorable exceptions) have not helped much. Instead of a body of critical assessment, Patchen has inspired what has too often been a cultist following, which has responded to his defiance and his physical suffering by making him into a martyr. Their Patchen is the dying Isaiah of Palo Alto, brought down by the inhuman forces of the

State, the Establishment, and the Vested Interests. There is enough truth in that analysis to keep one angry, but the polarization finally cheapens the serious issues about the literary life in the United States that Patchen's career raises. Patchen himself must bear some responsibility for the persistence of his personal legend, but insofar as his reputation is concerned he has been victimized by it far more than by any sinister institution his advocates have identified. His critics have had little trouble in turning aside charges of conspiracy and malice, and Patchen's work is rarely taught in college classrooms, discussed in literary journals, or anthologized.

In January 1972 Patchen died of heart failure after having been bedridden and in pain from back ailments off and on for thirty years.[4] A decade later, some of the personal resentments that contaminated responses to his work have been put to rest with him and his gift for trouble. Sometimes I feel that life has gone a little flat when I cannot get a colleague's back up with my argument for Kenneth Patchen. But the work remains—as uneven as ever—and I am still faced today with the question about the judiciousness of my choice of subjects that I had to consider in 1967. The corniness and stridency did not bother me much then, and, thinking it over, I guess they do not much bother me now. Patchen's shortcomings must modify our assessment of his work, but they should not determine it. Often they are simply to be accepted and enjoyed as correlatives of his strengths. Like most of the small, but intensely loyal audience Patchen has always claimed, I respond to an artist who has seemed to me incorruptible, who dedicated a difficult and painful life to the worship and nurture of the imagination, and who, despite the evidence of history, insisted always that there was in human nature something fine and bright and sure. He knew his mind, spoke out against mistrust and injustice, and championed, it seemed, some ancient marriage of flesh and spirit we had let ourselves forget. His was an often noble and powerful voice that called to community the waifs and runaways of two alienated generations. In all of this, he was a very heroic and lovely man. Although his stance and rhetoric could provoke his detractors to something resembling apoplexy, he could also elicit a spontaneous delight and affection from many readers who knew him only by one of his delicately erotic love poems, a whimsical illustrated limerick, or such eccentric masterpieces as *Memoirs of a Shy Pornographer*. We need not agree with or take pleasure from such a man—we are not obliged to like him—but we risk becoming fools and savages if we do not recognize his function in a complex culture and give him his due.

My professional reasons for returning to Patchen are as compelling as my personal ones. Questions of taste or loyalty aside, I continue to believe that he is an important writer in an important, often misvalued tradition. The legend that Patchen's adherents have fostered requires that he be unique and incomparable, and they have insisted with some energy that he can only be obscured or denigrated by attempts to associate him with other writers.[5] The attitude was encouraged by Patchen's own lofty sense of independence. "I was never influenced by anybody," he once grumpily announced to a friend.[6] While the egotism was perhaps necessary to the artist, it makes a bad model for the critic. Of course Patchen is unique. But to insist that he must be considered only on his own terms is defensive and finally self-defeating. Whether or not he himself appreciated it, he was a writer of time and place, "with antecedents," as Walt Whitman put it, in both his native traditions and a venerable strain of world literature. To discuss him in light of those traditions is one way of making his work accessible to his potentially large audience, clarifying some of his obscurities, and identifying the sort of norms by which he should be judged.

I also wish by studying Patchen to illuminate the definitive mysticism in the romantic literary tradition of Walt Whitman, to quarrel with unsympathetic explanations of its peculiarities, and to point to excellence that has not been fully recognized. Patchen is my representative man, but I discuss in detail other exemplars of the tradition when I feel that a direct approach to their work is called for. I believe that the tradition and the writers who enact it represent much of what is best in American life, that they embody the expansiveness of character and the altruism of motive that have been in eclipse in this country since the Civil War. I believe also that the failure of our culture to make better use of them is alarming.

Finally, I hope to add something to a collective definition of mysticism. The term is so often used and abused that I would despair of it if there were another word that would do as well. My purpose will be best accomplished by the scrutiny of my particular example, but I wish here to discuss briefly several general problems of definition and practice because I feel that they will have explanatory value in what follows.[7]

As I use the term, "mystical" applies to a personality type, a gift of perception, an openness to experience, a quality of expression. It is important that one be aware of the significance of the often radical differences among mystical systems, but I wish to concentrate here on those common elements of mystical personality that survive cultural determinism.[8] My usage is based on both Eastern and Western models and presupposes no belief in a God or any other article of religious faith. In fact, I am indifferent to matters of dogma except as they may interfere with a proper understanding of my subject. Mysticism is, finally, what mystics do, and it has as many valid manifestations as there are true mystics. I am interested in their character and behavior rather than the nature of their beliefs, although, of course, one is scarcely separable from the other. I wish also to emphasize that, as I use it, mysticism has no necessary connotation of superstition, asceticism, occultism, magic, unnatural sex, secret rites, narcotic intoxication, or trances. As far as I can tell, mystics are not particularly wild-eyed or ranting. In fact, they appear to be generally agreeable people, a little introverted perhaps, but good company. Many of them also seem to have a superior sense of humor.[9]

In religious communities mysticism has always been regarded as the highest form of spiritual science. In its largest sense, it is a way of life, art, and worship based upon an intuitive knowledge of mystery—the mystery of the nature of the universe, or God, or absolute reality. This knowledge is gained, without exception, by a direct experience that eludes the rational faculty—is, in fact, opposed to it—and, although sensed, is supersensory.[10] It is important to insist upon both the primacy and the privacy of experience for the mystic. Because of its loneliness, its both exhilarating and disturbing sense of isolation—"the flight of the Alone to the Alone," as Plotinus described it—the mystical experience contains within itself its own absolute authority, and is not subject to contradiction on any institutional or rationalistic terms. It is characterized by an emotion that consists inseparably of terror, strangeness, and exaltation, and by a state of awareness, heightened through insight into the processes of the universe until it is felt as a kind of omniscience. It is further characterized by what William James called "ineffability," the quality of being inaccessible to language and thus beyond the power of human beings to explain rationally to each other.[11]

Students of mysticism generally agree that while mystics are geniuses in applying it, the substance of the mystical experience is common to everyone. As Dean Inge explains, "mysticism has its origin in that which is the raw material of all religion, and perhaps of all philosophy and art as well, namely, the dim consciousness of the *beyond*, which is part of our nature as human beings."[12] Most of us regard that dim consciousness with suspicion and subordinate it to common sense. We experience the beyond as a vaguely shared identity, a participation in an ebullience of nature, a passing mood. The mystic, however, shapes the efforts of his entire life and the quality of each moment of consciousness to the things we distrust, and thus can enjoy a direct perception of the unity we only guess at. He experiences a wholeness, an integration of physical and spiritual, human and divine, subjective and objective, that confronts him with the eternal reality beneath the changing appearance of things.

The experience of union is the mystic's justification, and the insistence on unity is perhaps the most prominent common element of mysticism.[13] Mystics who attempt to describe their experience invariably claim that it is of the "All" or the "One." The unitive life as a consciously organic part of the pattern established by the supernatural is the final goal of mystic discipline.[14] Whatever the particular relationship of the individual soul to the One may be, the mystic sees clearly the identity of all created and uncreated things, the nature of being, from which all things are born and into which they return, and the harmonious interdependence of the natural and supernatural worlds. This mystical perception of unity and reality is made, mystics and scholars agree, through a "new sense,"[15] which apparently is a true vehicle of perception, but which transcends the familiar five senses, and breaks down the barriers among them. It is frequently described as a culmination of the worldly five.

Another fundamental characteristic of mysticism is the change occurring in what is perceived as the self. Although the new image of self varies according to various cosmologies, all mystics appear to agree that unity with supernature is approached by inculcating selflessness. In many Oriental religions and some of the nature mysticisms of the West, the notion of selflessness is based on the simple rejection of the concept of an ego, an "I" that persists in time and to which experience can be related. The idea that we can never again be the same self we are at each moment, that we cannot step twice in the same stream, is common enough to need no elaboration here.

In theistic mysticisms, the adept is required to abnegate his will completely in order to get beyond the limits of his own consciousness. As in the atheistic systems, such denial of self frees the individual for the infusion of the universal Self. Christian mystics have actually felt this process as a deification and been bold enough to describe it so.[16] Nontheistic mystics generally describe the infusion rather as the entrance of the universal into the individual.[17] It is important to notice here that although the authority of ego is denied, the idea of individuality is not. The self creates a point of reference for each experience and develops a continuum in time; freedom from that self releases the individual from the spiritual or psychological pressures of the past and future. However, an individual consciousness still exists in, and experiences, each moment. The awareness of one's individual body, also, and the recognition of the verbal convention by which human beings communicate are quite as acute among mystics as among others.

Such destructiveness toward one's individuality can have drastic consequences, and it exposes the mystic to the frightening possibilities of universal emptiness and spiritual failure. William James called this phenomenon the "diabolical mysticism."[18] When the mystic has managed to be rid of the self which imposes limitations, he is without identity, except that given him by his perceptions. In one sense, loss of identity is simply insanity, a danger mystics need to recognize. They would agree with Herman Melville's Ishmael (although without his sadness) that "man's insanity is heaven's sense," but they are also aware that the helplessness to which the mystic exposes himself forces him to cope with terrific infusions of reality or be broken by them. The risk is one every mystic must choose to run, and every mystic must submit to insanity, at least in the sense of disagreeing with the reality of one's neighbors, for a time.[19] The dark night of the soul, the paranoic and hallucinatory state of despair in the absence of the supernatural, is intrinsically part of the mystical process. It is the result of releasing supernatural power in the natural man, and the ascetic disciplines sometimes associated with mysticism are designed to give the individual a means by which to live with this power and keep his insanity from becoming permanent. Because of the dangers and terrors of the relationship between madness and illumination, mysticism is not monolithic in tone; it uses ominous language nearly as often as it does exalted poetry.

The serious problems of language and description created by such extremes of both positive and negative mystical emotion have led to common misconceptions that mysticism is some triumph of vague or murky thinking and that it is radically otherworldly. The rationalistic Fritz Staal, however, calls mysticism "a domain of the mind that appears to be as vast, varied, and intricate as many of the areas of physics."[20] It is saved from vagueness by being a way of life and action rather than philosophy or dogma, and because it is experience it has little use for abstraction. Josiah Royce maintained that "mystics are the only thoroughgoing empiricists in the history of philosophy."[21] All of their impulse is toward what to do rather than what to think. The unitive life is characteristically lived in a state of intense creative work.[22] That emphasis on action informs alike the political career of Catherine of Siena and the philosophy of the Bhagavad-Gita, which develops as a response to the scruples of its Everyman, Arjuna, against action, and which fits the quietistic and aristocratic mysticism of the Upanishads to the demands of life in society.

Such suggestions of public heroism, however, exaggerate the idea of what mysticism typically is: the art of day-to-day life in its minutest detail. In a famous Zen story it is the ability to notice if an umbrella is placed to the left or the right of the footwear.[23] For

Julian of Norwich it is the discovery of God's love in "a little thing, the quantity of an hazel-nut."[24] The perception that has been heightened by experience of the absolute is returned to the world of the senses, and the miraculous is seen in the commonplace. "How curious! how real!/ Underfoot the divine soil, overhead the sun," writes Walt Whitman in "Starting from Paumanok," and his celebration of the wonder in reality parallels so closely the words of the Zen adept P'ang Yun, "How wondrously supernatural,/ And how miraculous this!/ I draw water, and I carry fuel,"[25] that if one didn't know better, he might assume a direct line of influence. This attention to everyday life is more pronounced in Eastern than in Western mysticisms, but it is true of all mystics that the texture and gesture of their lives are subtly but radically changed. A remarkable Taoist cook, described in the *Chuang Tzu*, had in nineteen years butchered several thousand oxen with the same knife, yet by application of the Tao of butchery—that is, meticulous attention to every detail of the work—"I deal with it in a spirit-like manner, and do not look at it with my eyes. The use of my senses is discarded, and my spirit acts as it wills." Furthermore, his knife never needed replacement or sharpening. His monarch "heard the words of [his] cook, and learned from them the nourishment of our life."[26]

In turning our attention from mysticism itself to its literature, we can say, first, that a mystical writer is one who characteristically makes the mystical experience, its emotion, and the perceptions of the new sense the basis of his art and the artistic personality he exploits in his writing. Most poets have a trace of the mystic in them; the mystical poet isolates it, develops it, and builds a career on it. Basic questions of identification can be more troublesome than they might seem, but for purposes of literary inquiry, this professional impulse, rather than biographical concerns, must be definitive.

After that, mystical literature confronts us chiefly with problems of intelligibility and rhetoric. All experience that is not itself verbal experience is finally inaccessible to language, and mystical experience is radically so—is, in fact, antagonistic to language. The mystical attitude is illustrated by the *Tao Te Ching* (or *Lao*

Tzu), which begins with a discussion of words and the observation, in James Legge's translation, that "the name that can be named is not the enduring and unchanging name." It follows, then, in Lao Tzu's most famous epigram, that "he who knows does not speak; he who speaks does not know."[27] If one takes the roguish Lao Tzu at face value, of course, the implications of his utterance involve the reader in some verbal equivalent of infinite regression—a little like staring too intently at the Indian girl on the box of Land O Lakes butter. His standoff between theory and practice, however, illustrates a typical paradox of mystical literature. Language is suspect because it leads one to mistake verbal conventions or mental constructs for things. It can be used to protect consciousness from reality. On the other hand, language is a basic tool, and mystical writers have always attempted to use it to transcend its own limitations. Zen Buddhism, for example, has developed in addition to nonverbal techniques a number of teaching methods based on one-upmanship and non sequiturs, creating by the way a raffish anecdotal literature of the spirit. A delightful response by the Zen master Ummon to the question of a student (the exercise is called *mondo*) is illustrative: "This pupil went to Ummon and asked the same question ['All Buddhas of the ten parts of the universe enter the one road of Nirvana. Where does that road begin?']. Ummon, who happened to have a fan in his hand, said: 'This fan will reach to the thirty-third heaven and hit the nose of the presiding deity there. It is like the Dragon Carp of the Eastern Sea tipping over the rain-cloud with his tail.'"[28] Such abuse of language attempts to bring two or more contradictory systems of knowledge together so that they are experienced at once, thus exciting an approximation of nonverbalizable knowledge in the reader or auditor.[29] D. T. Suzuki explains: "If the system of logic that has been in circulation is found inadequate to explain away the *satori* [enlightenment] experience and the *mondo* that has grown from it, the philosopher will have to invent a new system of thinking to fit the experience, and not conversely, that is, to disprove the empirical fact by means of logic."[30]

Extremes of semantic irrationality, however, are rare outside of the literature of Zen itself. More frequently mystical writers confront us with an unusual reliance on paradox and synesthesia, and, in particular, special varieties of metaphor and symbol. The metaphors of mysticism are consistently strange and disturbing, even when they are drawn from radically different theologies. Darkness, for instance, is used in all mysticisms with similarly ambiguous reference: first, as the color of evil and deprivation, the unknown and the sinister, but also as a warm, moist darkness, pregnant with the divine, and remaining dark only because of our inability to open our eyes to supernatural light. Hence the astonishing extremes of ecstasy and torment in immediate proximity in Saint John of the Cross's poem and treatise, *The Dark Night of the Soul*.

Because he wants some naked language to express his new reality, the mystic is frustrated by his reliance on metaphor and often the strain shows. Fire, the big hunter cats, angels, sexual union, pilgrimage; all take on heightened and evocative substance, and often unnatural juxtaposition, in the hallucinatory atmosphere of the mystical poem. Orthodox Christians have a traditional evocative imagery of their own,[31] a sort of literary presence of the Paraclete, which can be raided for otherwise unverbalizable responses, but even these are dangerous. Saint John of the Cross discusses the problem in the prologue to his *Spiritual Canticle*:

> For who can write down that which He reveals to loving souls wherein He dwells? And who can set forth in words that which He makes them to feel? And lastly, who can express that which He makes them to desire? Of a surety, none; nay, indeed, not the very souls through whom He passes. And it is for this reason that, by means of figures, comparisons and similitudes, they allow something of that which they feel to overflow and utter secret mysteries from the abundance of the Spirit, rather than explain these things rationally. These similitudes, if they be not read with the simplicity of the spirit of love and understanding embodied in them, appear to be nonsense rather than the expression of reason, as may be seen in the divine Songs of Solomon and in other books of the Divine Scripture, where, since the Holy Spirit cannot express the abundance of His meaning in

> common and vulgar terms, He utters mysteries in strange
> figures and similitudes. Whence it follows that no words of
> holy doctors, despite all that they have said and may yet say,
> can ever expound these things fully, neither could they be
> expounded in words of any kind. That which is expounded
> of them, therefore, is ordinarily the least part of that which
> they contain.[32]

If they are not read by a creative reader, then, strange figures can
seem insane, as many poets—Saint John of the Cross included—
have learned. The condition not only endangers the poet; it places
a great responsibility upon the reader not to be hurried or in-
sensitive.

Readers are asked to assume similar responsibilities in confront-
ing the issue of how and what the symbology of mystical literature
means. There is a patristic sense in which the word "mystical"
means "allegorical"—Saint John of the Cross clearly has that
meaning in mind—and Christian mystical literature tends to accu-
mulate exegesis and proliferate meanings. In a theology, mystical
experience belongs to a class of universal significations that can be
interpreted according to type and precedent. On the other hand,
there is an absolute self-centeredness to mystical symbolism,
which makes it impossible to interpret at all. Because each mysti-
cal experience contains its own authority and justification, its
symbols have no external referent. They are literally and only
what they are in the poem or treatise. Any reader of William
Blake's prophetic works will recognize the danger of obscurity this
quality of symbolism provokes. That maddening privacy is the
meaning of Walt Whitman's much maligned "I too am untrans-
latable," and it led Saint John of the Cross to stress the final
elusiveness of his strange figures. The reader, in turn, is in effect
required to re-create by imagination and empathy the mystical
experience of the author so that the context of his imagery and
symbolism may be intuitively felt and applied. The demand is not
much like that of such self-reflexive postmodern authors as Vladi-
mir Nabokov and John Barth that a reader be sufficiently ac-
quainted with them and their works to appreciate private jokes and
personal allusions. Rather it is a moral demand for Saint John of

the Cross's "simplicity of the spirit of love and understanding." The reader may legitimately reject it, be indifferent to it, or feel unable to comply, but unless he attempts to meet it, he renounces all right of access to the special literary languages mysticism has developed.

The mystical artifact, then, assumes an unusual degree of complicity by the reader in the creative act—a "gymnast's struggle," in Walt Whitman's words. The condition not only creates textual difficulty, it also emphasizes an important point in the definition of mystical writing. Although there are many exceptions, the dominant vision of literary art in the West has been the static "made object," the creation that like John Donne's "well-wrought urn" exists, finally, apart from both its creator and its audience, sufficient unto itself. It aspires to perfection—that is, completion—and to the degree that it approaches the perfect it can be abstracted and paraphrased. It offers essentially the same text to every reader. Mystical writing, however, assumes that the artifact is a process of creation in which the growth of form and the sensation of beauty present themselves uniquely to each individual, that art is a relationship between each reader and the artist. It aspires not to perfection but to illumination and new beginnings. It accommodates change and not only celebrates but also requires the sometimes messy interchange between, and final inseparability of, art and life. It insists that art is rather to be used than simply observed. We might find models of this aspect of mystical literature in the Chinese book of divination *I Ching* (*Classic of Changes*), whose title in part gives it away, and which has no real text until a reader consults it, interprets it, and applies it,[33] or in such spiritual manuals as the Tibetan *Book of the Dead*, which assumes that the audience (the dead or dying person) is literally discovering and enacting the text. Japanese haiku has also been described as an art based on the satori experience that relies on an intuitive interchange between poet and reader for its validity.[34] Closer to home, Henry Miller's *Tropic of Capricorn* affords an unusually nice imaging of the peculiar materials, structures, and relationships of the mystical text: "I relate these incidents briefly and hurriedly as they flash through my mind; my memory is packed with thousands of such details, with a myriad faces, gestures, tales, confessions all entwined and interlaced like the stupendous reeling facade of some Hindu temple made not of stone but of the experience of human flesh, a monstrous dream edifice built entirely of reality and yet not reality itself but merely the vessel in which the mystery of the human being is contained."[35]

Acknowledgments

I would like to thank David Levin for his advice and encouragement in this project over the years. I have also been helped greatly by Miriam Patchen, Joel Climenhaga, Thomas C. Moser, Albert Gelpi, Austin Quigley, Johnny Holdren, Donald Sheehy, and a number of noisy, intolerant partisans of Patchen, who keep a critic on his toes. The University of Virginia Summer and Small Grants committees assisted me financially. I wish I had time and space enough to list, for justice's sake, the names of those who attempted to discourage me.

Kenneth Patchen

and American Mysticism

Chapter I

An American Mysticism

*A special verse for you—a flash of duty long neglected—your
  mystic roll strangely gather'd here*
                    —Whitman, "A Twilight Song"

The history of mysticism and its literature in the United States
follows a typical pattern of migration, adaptation, and change.
Like many American ideas and institutions, it was borrowed from
the past, secularized, mixed eclectically with other ideas, and
applied to the American sense of identity and mission. Its institu-
tional character in older societies was either abandoned or became
suspect in the institutional structure of a culture which was self-
consciously ridding itself of foreign orthodoxies, and it survived
only incidentally as a way of religious knowledge and action.

Mysticism came to America with the Puritan settlers of New
England as an implicit and mistrusted minor element of their
Calvinist theology.[1] It haunts those doctrines of Calvinism that
emphasize the personal experience of conversion, as it does any
system in which the individual soul's relationship with the deity is
a matter of subjective rather than ritual justification. Like many
Protestant sects, Puritanism leaned toward spirit mysticism, in
which the dictates of the inner voice, as an expression of the
indwelling divinity, are given authority beyond scriptural or doc-
trinal limitation. Although the insistence on both the examination
and authority of the steadfast individual conscience gives New
England Puritanism much of its disciplined strength, orthodox
Calvinists were never comfortable with such potentially antino-
mian attitudes. Once the idea of an inner impulse corresponding to
the will of God was allowed, there was no logical way of limiting

its influence. The Puritans were alert to the dangers of solipsism and to the treacherous ways of Satan, who used subjective illumination for his own ends. Moreover, the conviction that one possessed one's own best authority threatened the social experiment of putting spiritual truth to work in the world. Both dangers are illustrated by the career of Anne Hutchinson and the uproar she caused in the Bay Colony. Consequently, antinomianism became the chief American heresy. The authority of the individual relationship with God was checked by the congregation, and the emotional excitement of direct communication with the supernatural was suppressed, or at least discouraged. Although such a religious genius as Jonathan Edwards could later recapture much of the mystical impulse of early Puritanism, and although the Puritan community could be briefly aroused by the Great Awakening, the general Puritan distrust of experience beyond the control of the church became increasingly typical of the New England establishment.

As a characteristic of reform Protestantism, the priority of mystical experience continued to be emphasized by the Quakers, who had their own problems of control in their early days, but in whom the development of quietism and the moderating influence of the meeting cooled the more fiery manifestations of the spirit. As a philosophical and emotional element in the intellectual history of New England, mysticism is most commonly expressed in theological variations on the theme of divine indwelling in both human and physical nature.[2] However, the most important survival of the Puritan mystical impulse is probably much more general and more difficult to define. Its urgency becomes identified with the political element of the Puritan's "errand into the wilderness" and, subsequently, with the American preoccupation with national purpose. In the United States, that sense of the "beyond" which Dean Inge located at the roots of mystical experience has traditionally been a sense of something close at hand. The beyond has been over the next hill—in Kentucky or Utah or California—and Americans have inclined to identify their country, at least potentially, with the biblical promised lands. The search for this physically proximate beyond, the westering after it, creates one of the informing myths of our literature.

The history of mysticism in America, then, at least as a literary phenomenon, is in one sense the history of the transformation and diffusion of a discipline rather than of transmission to successive generations. Orthodox literary mystics have either remained obscure, like Jones Very, the Concord quietist who has always been overshadowed by his colorful transcendentalist neighbors, or else felt out of place, like T. S. Eliot, the reactionary admirer of patristic Christianity and occasionally mystical poet of *Four Quartets*, who early in his career left the United States permanently. Even Edgar Allan Poe, whose visions of an ideal beauty are related to Neoplatonic mysticisms, has a more secure critical reputation abroad than among his countrymen, who still often regard him alternately as a raving drug fiend and a storyteller for children. Poe, Eliot, and Very also belong in their interests and personalities to a past which more fully American mystical writers have rejected. They are decadent by native standards because of their preoccupation with sin and the fallen state of humanity.

It is clear, moreover, that we call Poe and Eliot mystical poets only by stretching definitions uncomfortably thin. Both writers are only occasionally mystical in their interests, and both have a marked tendency to fall back on rationalistic discourse and the analytic faculty. A similar distinction might be made with regard to Herman Melville and Emily Dickinson, whom John E. Jacoby considered as mystics in the first book-length study of American mysticism.[3] Although they were obviously excited by the prospect of mystical union, Melville and Dickinson seem to have feared particularly the potential madness in the necessary loss of self and to have withdrawn on the verge of surrendering to the enthralling but terrible "other." Their reliance on defensive irony and the suspiciousness with which they considered the Emersonian transcendentalism to which they were attracted define their ambivalence. More defensible examples of orthodox mystical writers might include, in our century, Thomas Merton and Brother Antoninus, both Catholic monks who attracted a considerable audience. And there is no telling how many mystical souls—Catholic, Quaker, Jewish, or whatever—have lived and died unpublished. Perhaps the most advanced mystics have no need to record their experience. Be that as it may, the possibility that European orthodoxies may survive in the United States does not invalidate the contention that the country is largely hostile to them. After the passing of the ascetic Calvinism in which the Mathers, Jonathan Edwards, and Edward Taylor found expression, the demands of American society made difficult—one is tempted to say outlawed —the monkish training mystics have developed as a way of harnessing supernatural power. At least in the nineteenth and early twentieth centuries Protestant America would consider such activity popish—wickedly Spanish or Italian. Merton and Antoninus owed their currency more to their mastery of certain literary and cultural idioms than to their Catholicism, and that they are our examples of traditional mysticism simply points to the relative lack of that interest in American life and letters. Merton in particular developed two nearly mutually exclusive audiences, one as a Catholic thinker, another as an avant-garde writer, and he often expressed his religious attitudes according to the modes and vocabulary of the native mysticism, with which, particularly later in his life, he allied himself politically and as an artist. Born in France, educated in part in England, a spiritual citizen of a community whose loyalties hearkened back to even more foreign times and places, he made himself into a characteristic American. He is an anomaly, but an instructive one.

So much for the traditions of European mysticism in America.[4] Perhaps because no adequate older way was readily available, there arose a native literary mysticism which found expression in the particulars of American history and culture, and which is the definitive American mysticism. It can be distinguished first in Ralph Waldo Emerson's rediscovery of the potential for wonder in the heterodox ideas of God and nature that he worked out of his New England heritage. After Emerson, the mystical company includes, to greater or lesser degree: Henry David Thoreau, Walt Whitman, William Carlos Williams, Waldo Frank, Jean Toomer, Hart Crane, Thomas Wolfe, Henry Miller, Kenneth Patchen, Theodore Roethke, and, among more recent writers, Allen Ginsberg and Gary Snyder. One might expand the list to include the John Steinbeck of the remarkably Emersonian *Sea of Cortez* (although we must beware of attributing the Emersonianism exclusively to Steinbeck),[5] Van Wyck Brooks (as a theoretician, before

1920),[6] and Lewis Mumford, especially in *The Conduct of Life*. Thomas Merton is a special case. The theological and philosophical assumptions of the group I have isolated were largely foreign to him, but he wrote exemplary texts in their language.

Even among these many names we find few rigorously mystical personalities, but the few we do find are strong individuals of major literary achievement. The group also includes a number of mystical philosophers, who have based a more or less intellectual philosophical system on limited mystical experience—either their own or their literary antecedents'. I would count Whitman, Patchen, Miller, Roethke, and possibly even Williams as representative mystical personalities.[7] Frank and Brooks are certainly mystical philosophers. In any case, all of these individuals (excepting, of course, Merton) share a monistic nature mysticism, which can be either theistic or atheistic according to individual temperament. That is, although some writers talk about a god, they distinguish it neither from the physical nature which is its manifestation nor from themselves. In a monistic universe that is also a theistic universe everyone is God. When it is both theistic and monistic, and to the extent that it is both, the cosmology of American mysticism resembles that of the Upanishads, in which the divine being is compared to a substance, pervading the universe as salt pervades water, and in which "Thou art That" pervasive substance.

Despite its expansiveness, that cosmic identity does not go so far beyond that it becomes vague or unapproachable. As in most mystical disciplines, it expresses itself in the specific world to which we all have access. The cosmic identity is an American identity and an individual identity as well. The particular self is America, is all humanity, is nature. That immediate relevance of the individual to any other concern makes personality a more serious consideration than it is for philosophies in which the self is sharply limited by natural or environmental circumstances. The individual personality, developed to its full potential, leads America toward the fulfillment of history, and defines our new world, with its new perceptions and hopes. It is that heroic personality which American mystical writers characteristically invoke.[8] Belief in the cosmic significance of the self cannot, of course, be attributed equally to all of the writers I have grouped. The mature William Carlos Williams, for instance, never speculated about a cosmic identity. But even Williams seems to feel that his identification is complete despite its refusal to expand very far—that it includes all of the cycle of life and death and change that exists in any important sense.

Although the extension of the self into both physical nature and the selves of other human beings is basic to several religious systems and would probably have invited dogmatic definition in another culture, American mystical writers have generally remained secular. In fact, they have often been openly antagonistic to institutional religion and have acquired reputations as infidels and blasphemers. Ralph Waldo Emerson's exile from Harvard College is only the first example of orthodox reaction to the American mysticism, and Emerson's is still one of the least frightening of mystical reputations. More important, the firmly secular orientation of these writers reinforces the mystical return of supernatural experience to the familiar world, so that the quality of everyday things is heightened. One of the wonderfully solid lines in American poetry is the first line of Emerson's "Hamatraya," which consists of nothing but commonplace Anglo-Saxon patronymics—"Bulkeley, Hunt, Willard, Hosmer, Meriam, Flint." Indeed, all these writers can be identified by their ability to release immense amounts of energy into contemplation of mundane detail, which is often presented without restraint or fastidiousness. One thinks of Walt Whitman's celebration of the "scent of these arm-pits" or Henry Miller's descriptions of wet genitalia.

The secularization of the mystical impulse also results in the vision of a natural rather than a supernatural unitive life. Like all mystics, American mystical writers envisage the unitive state as one of great creative activity, but they value action and its results more for their own sake than as service to God. In practice, the vision of the unitive life in nature merged with the social vision of evolutionary progress and produced a strong utopian theme in the work of many mystical writers. The utopian impulse is reflected both in such writings as Whitman's *Democratic Vistas* and Gary Snyder's *Regarding Wave* and in such practical attempts to live the unitive life as the transcendentalist Brook Farm experiment and Henry Thoreau's stay at Walden.

The consistently secular quality of American mysticism is largely a result of the eclecticism that is another major characteristic of both the literary mode and national culture itself. As good Americans, mystical writers have borrowed heavily but selectively from a range of Western and Oriental cultures, and until Merton and Gary Snyder, who often writes as a Zen Buddhist, none of them had made extensive use of any single system. The Western mystical tradition that our writers have exploited is a Platonic tradition, especially as expressed in nineteenth-century German idealism and transcendentalism. It is also a Christian tradition, from which American mystical writers have taken, first, some of the rhythms and imagery—and, often, the fiery prophetic stance—of the King James Version of the Old Testament. The Bible, especially in its poetic books, is an important source not only for language but also for a typical attitude of these writers, who often felt that they were inscribing the scriptures of their own days and lands. The mystical strain in the native Puritanism, a suspect ideology to most of our writers, has been assimilated only indirectly and unawares.

The important Christianity for most American literary mystics has been, of course, Protestant, and particularly Quaker. Anglo-Saxon mistrust of all things Roman Catholic excluded at least earlier writers from exposure to that most sustained tradition of Western mysticism, which, with its emphasis on introspection, was considered morbid. On the other hand, the Quaker deemphasis of dogma and respect for the authority of the inner light have impressed writers who are not themselves believers as analogous to the condition of illumination. The meeting, which replaced formally structured services, has seemed admirably democratic. Furthermore, the Quakers left an indelible mark on Walt Whitman, the most representative and influential of American mystical writers. In his long essay on Elias Hicks, the Quaker reformer and evangelist, Whitman described the inner light as the essence of religion and morality; and in a perceptive essay, D. Elton Trueblood has suggested that Hicks's influence may extend even to Whitman's characteristic line and rhythm.[9] Whitman was not the first to praise the Quakers or to use them as representative Americans, but through him their plain speech, calm stability, and fierce attention to conscience became a permanent part of an ideal. The figure of the modest, thoughtful Quaker, who follows his inner convictions into action, has become, explicitly or not, a model for the American among writers who have succeeded Whitman.

The Western sources of the American mystical tradition are routinely identified in studies of American romanticism and transcendentalism, and they need no further elucidation here. There is some danger, however, that they may be overemphasized. The legacy of the West is only part of the background on which these writers draw, and it is limited, or even distorting, as a means of explaining their art, because they are often closer in attitude and expression to the East, which provides them especially with an ideal of cosmic personality. The discovery of an absolute personal identity in a universe without God establishes the ground of their philosophies and the chief responses to the problems of their world. It has, for instance, suggested a definition of reality by which the troublesome question of the relationship between subjectivity and objectivity has been answered. American mystics also borrowed from Asia the assumption of an essential congruity of action and contemplation. The belief that these are simply two aspects of the same human activity argues for the spiritual worth of a vigorous American life. It can also be developed further in the idea of making one's life a work of art—living so that contemplation is expressed in every action, so that the inner being complements and is in harmony with each gesture of the physical self. Even Thomas Merton acknowledged the power and attractiveness of such attitudes in the Oriental researches of his last years.

The Eastern texts that had the greatest influence during the nineteenth century were the Upanishads and the Bhagavad-Gita. Because they were the examples of Eastern wisdom to which Emerson, Thoreau, and possibly Whitman were first exposed, their impact was more emotionally satisfying and perhaps more lasting than if they had been part of a Western tradition. Representing a new, exotic discovery of truth, they appealed more to the transcendental imagination than to the intellect, and probably constituted also a gesture of defiance toward the Christian United States. Emerson and Thoreau tended to read the Upanishads and Gita superficially, and to borrow large chunks of convenient philosophy without considering the specific conditions that made the philosophy valid. Asian concepts were thus often too easily applied to American life. Emerson's justly prized poem "Brahma" is representative of his general, though noble, failure to capture fully the substance of the Eastern texts he wished to adapt to American thought. With its initial inspiration probably in an aphorism from the Katha Upanishad—"If the slayer think that he slays, if the slain think that he is slain, neither of them knows the truth. The self slays not, nor is he slain"[10]—the poem is an accurate statement of basic Vedanta (although one might find in the final stanza too strong a hint of Western dualism). It is also an excellent expression of that imaginative grandeur which New England Brahmins found in the Indian scriptures. But it remains too much a statement of an abstract truth which has not been derived from experience and which has no particular application. Emerson's restatement of Indian mysticism is more satisfactory in such poems as "Hamatraya," in which mystical truth is expressed in terms of the familiar American life he himself urged upon his countrymen. The philosophical success Emerson may have wrung from the Vedas is, however, less important than the currency he gave them. Vedantic monism and insistence on the divinity of the self persist and are characteristic of American literary mysticism even today.

The Upanishads and the Gita were probably the only mystical Eastern texts the transcendentalists knew; they seem but dimly aware of the principles of Buddhism and ignorant about Taoism. Something of the legendary career of Lao Tzu was known to the essayist E. G. Holland as early as 1852 (he calls the sage Lautsee and "the great Transcendentalist of China"), but Holland's description seems based only on confused hearsay.[11] It is unfortunate that Emerson, Thoreau, and Whitman later did not have access to the *Tao Te Ching*, because its evocations of the universal "Way" of nature might have widened their own, and Thoreau especially would have found congenial the philosophical anarchism of Lao Tzu. Some later writers did make important use of Taoism— notably Henry Miller, who included the *Tao Te Ching* in the list of major influences he appended to *The Books in My Life*. Miller is like the Taoists in his devotion to naturalness, his hedonistic insistence on living from moment to moment, and his rejection of social responsibility. Thomas Merton, who possessed none of those qualities, nevertheless translated the *Chuang Tzu*.

Zen Buddhism, which historically derives in part from Taoism, has also become important in American mysticism, but more often for its parallels to, and illuminations of, American practice than for any direct line of transmission. In recent years, it has surfaced as the philosophy of Gary Snyder, who studied in Japanese monasteries, as an influence on Thomas Merton, and as one of the many Oriental interests of Allen Ginsberg, but it occurs more often simply as a striking similarity of character or a quality of perception. Walt Whitman, for instance, could have known nothing about it, but is described by Robert H. Blyth, in his masterfully eccentric *Zen in English Literature and Oriental Classics*, as having "a great deal of Zen scattered through his writings."[12] Further, the most consistently revealing expression of Zen in American literature is probably to be found in the work of William Carlos Williams, who also would not have known about it until relatively late in his career. Several Japanese Buddhists had been working and publishing in the United States since the 1890s,[13] but Zen did not become an intellectual force in the West until the appearance of D. T. Suzuki's first series of *Essays in Zen Buddhism* in 1927. In ways that at times seem almost uncanny, Williams exemplifies many of the characteristics of Zen's atheistic nature mysticism, and his famous dictum, "no ideas except in things," is as close to an aphoristic summary of Zen as one is likely to find. J. Hillis Miller's description of the egolessness that the poet experiences before physical reality and the "at oneness" he feels with it—a state at which he says Williams arrived through intuition[14]—is, so far as I can tell, a description of the essential Zen experience. Williams's own concept of the artist as an extension of nature in *Spring and All*,[15] his responsiveness to the radiance of the commonplace or trivial (the fragmented green glass in "Behind Walls"), and his ability to capture the moment without needing to explain it (as in "Proletarian Portrait") are all characteristic Zen qualities. The representation of himself as the clownish, antiintellectual doctor that he exploits throughout his work is also functionally similar to the flippant attitudes toward oneself in which Zen delights. Perhaps the best sense of Williams's relationship to Zen, however, can be evoked by quoting Ch'ing-yuan's famous description of his spiritual experience: "Before I had studied Zen for thirty years, I saw mountains as mountains, and waters as waters. When I arrived at a more intimate knowledge, I came to the point where I saw that mountains are not mountains, and waters are not waters. But now that I have got its very substance I am at rest. For it's just that I see mountains once again as mountains, and waters once again as waters."[16]

Beyond such substantial contributions and parallels from the traditional philosophies of both East and West, the eclecticism of American mystical writers has expressed itself in their use of such exotic systems as Swedenborgianism, theosophy, the Sufism that interested Emerson, and the work of the Russian occultist, P. D. Ouspensky, whose *Tertium Organum* fascinated Hart Crane and had a strong influence on the symbolism of *The Bridge*. Other noteworthy borrowings include surrealism, which is itself suspect as a mysticism,[17] but is a system that has developed visionary techniques that mystics can exploit, and the similarly neo-Freudian metaphysics of Dr. Wilhelm Reich, a German scientist-mystic who claimed to have discovered the principle of cosmic energy, and who died in an American prison after his controversial conviction for medical fraud. After listing these sometimes dubious sources, and considering the quantity and intensity of borrowings from other cultures, it is disappointing, if not particularly surprising, that until Gary Snyder's *Myths and Texts* no one had made extensive literary use of the native mysticism of the American Indian. Still, the range of mystical eclecticism is impressive. Kenneth Patchen, for example, was stimulated by such diverse influences as the Old Testament prophets, especially Isaiah and Jeremiah, William Blake and other European literary mystics, the *I Ching*, classic Buddhism and Taoism, Zen, spiritual alchemy (specifically the *Splendor Solis* of the mysterious Solomon Trismosin), and surrealism—all this in addition to the American background.[18]

The eclecticism is easily established, but its effects are not so easily judged. In a culture that has a firm traditional way of thought, the adaptation of ideas from another culture changes slightly a pattern already set—that is, the change and its effects can be more or less surely seen in reference to the tradition. Americans, however—mystics and others—tend to borrow ideas wholesale from a great many cultures and put them together in a sort of spiritual montage. The result cannot always be clearly compared to anything that has previously existed, although some of its effects can be isolated. On the positive side, the very wildness of some American juxtapositions of ideas is stimulating, and the violent break with the past and its beliefs can be liberating. Such developments have evolved among mystical writers a literary stance that emphasizes originality, daring, and a determination to get beyond the traditional limits of literature and express what was once inexpressible. In a sense, the iconoclasm and sometimes strident insistence on freedom have done just what they were intended to do. They have invoked new truths and initiated new forms.

The fulfillment of such revolutionary aspirations has established a satisfyingly paradoxical tradition of antitradition. "The only way to be like Whitman," William Carlos Williams asserted, "is to write *unlike* Whitman. Do I expect to be a companion to Whitman by mimicking his manners? I might even so please some old dotard, some 'good grey poet' by kow-towing to him; but not Whitman—or if I did please Whitman I would not please myself. Let me at least realize that to be a poet one must be himself!"[19] Williams's statement is noteworthy for its camaraderie and for the way in which his disclaimer of Whitman's authority shows how faithfully he respects Whitman's example.

Such are the benefits of eclecticism. They define a major American mystical endeavor. The deficiencies of eclecticism, however, compromise it to the extent that it cannot be considered among the first rank of world mysticisms. Like Americans in general, the mystical writers have been too selective. They have often ignored the complexities of the philosophies upon which they have drawn and have sometimes been insensitive to the toughmindedness that ennobles many classic mysticisms. For instance, the idea of progressive evolution across lifetimes, which American mystics may have had from the Bhagavad-Gita before they heard of Darwin, and which they used to justify their great optimism, is balanced in Eastern texts by the doctrine of karma.

Karma is simply the law of cause and effect—that an individual or a people must act out the consequences of choice and behavior, even in other incarnations. Evolution according to karma is not necessarily positive, but is determined by momentum from the past. It clearly disallows any notion of escaping history. Although the theory of karmic impulsion seems to have been current among nineteenth-century American mystical writers, it did not much influence their practice. Emerson recognized karma somewhat confusedly in his doctrine of compensation,[20] and Whitman appears to describe it in his discussion of inevitable consequence in the preface to the 1855 *Leaves of Grass*. Neither man, however, was able to incorporate the idea he outlined into his emotional makeup. In the same essay in which he described karma, Whitman affirmed that "the eternal tendencies of all toward happiness make the only point of sane philosophy," and this alogical optimism is also notoriously characteristic of Emerson.

Such weaknesses are too common. In fact, the freedom of American mystical writers to accept any idea that strikes the imagination has led to a distinct inclination to traffic in the occult or second-rate. The fault can be seen in Walt Whitman's interest in phrenology, Henry Miller's inability to distinguish between Lao Tzu and Madame Blavatsky, and even William Carlos Williams's temporary acquiescence to Ezra Pound's version of social credit. The willingness of many mystical writers to accept any system, far-fetched or not, that offers a complete solution to philosophical problems is, in one sense, a tribute to their determination to find truth in whatever trappings it may be hidden. But it also can result in sloppy thinking.

Finally, their eclecticism denied American mystical writers a single orthodox tradition by which they might be guided through their entire experience. In his introduction to the works of Saint John of the Cross, E. Allison Peers says that the great strength of the saint was that he had prepared himself in "dogmatic theology" as well as "mystical theology," and that he avoided excess by testing his mystical perception against the teaching of the church.[21] The language and values Peers uses are, of course, those of a Catholic hagiographer, but his categories may be extended beyond their strictly theological context. Saint John, entering upon the crucial experience of his life, had the help of all the Christian mystics who had preceded him to tell him what was happening to him and bring him through the unknown trials he faced. A similar, if more primitive, guide was established by the Quakers, who tamed much of the wild behavior that had troubled their early days by instituting the meeting, at which the promptings of the inner light were tested against the collective wisdom of the congregation. But, as Malcolm Cowley has noted,[22] Walt Whitman had no dogmatic theology to tell him that he might be mistaking a side effect of the mystical experience for divine inspiration. In effect, Whitman encountered his mystical self as if he were the first mystic. Such spiritual individualism is dangerous because energy is released without disciplines to channel it, and the new sense of illumination and freedom is not always properly directed. Whitman found the strength in himself to survive, but others have been either weaker or less fortunate. Herman Melville investigated the problem of undisciplined mystical expression in the insanity of his monomaniacal characters: Taji, Ahab, and Pierre Glendinning. Yvor Winters brought evidence, as it were, to Melville's insight by tracing similarly destructive aspects of transcendentalism in particular in the career and suicide of Hart Crane.[23]

Whatever the philosophical shortcomings of American mysticism, it has given rise to an important and robust literature, and as literature it will finally be judged. Among writers, the mystical impulse is shaped by the particularities of time and place, and American national life has become a metaphor for the working out of mystical imperatives. From the vantage point of unitive knowledge, America represents moral regeneration, responsibility, and a new way of perception.

The literary tradition of mysticism in the United States is first fully expressed in the work of Walt Whitman. His predecessors, Emerson and Thoreau, are closely related to the tradition he established, but they are too emotionally reserved and dependent on the intellect to be truly mystics. Many of those who come after Whitman also stand apart in one particular or another, although it is true of them, as of the transcendentalists, that most of the generalizations made about Whitman's tradition apply. If they are not always mystics they are always romantics, and their American mystical tradition is, in one sense, simply one extreme manifestation of the romantic tradition. In fact, as a literary phenomenon, mysticism can be considered a subcategory of romanticism, differing in the intensity rather than the nature of its fundamental assumptions. It possesses certain literary characteristics that, in addition to the traits already discussed, give it a separate artistic identity:

(1) American literary mysticism emphasizes innocence. Human nature, according to mystical writers, is essentially good and trustworthy, or is at least capable of perfection. Although they recognize the fact of evil, they are not tolerant of the argument that it is a part of the fundamental nature of things. Even such later writers as Patchen, who write in great agony about the evil in the world, are tortured more by their perception that it is a disturbance of natural order than by any belief in innate depravity.

The insistence on human goodness and perfectibility defines even the first impulses of American literary mysticism—as witnessed by Perry Miller's remark distinguishing Emerson from the earlier traditions of New England, that he was "an Edwards in whom the concept of original sin had evaporated."[24] We might notice also that disbelief in the fall of human nature marks perhaps the basic distinction between Eastern and Western thought. The idea that humanity is by nature less than perfectible has never occurred to Oriental mystics, whose Edens and Utopias have consequently been free of the fictional connotations that are necessarily provoked by such visions in the West.

(2) It attempts to define and create the hero. Heroism—the defense of the values of one's society in one's own person—is associated by American mystical writers with the career of the poet, who is a sort of prophet-priest, and lives the mystical unitive life in terms of American democracy, thus providing both a model and a challenge for his countrymen. By incarnating democratic values and destiny, and giving them literary expression, he establishes their force in the physical world.

The idea of the poet as mystical priest and hero becomes permanently important in American literature with Emerson's essay, "The Poet" (1844), even though Emerson's discussion of the bardic hero clearly provides him more with a theoretical than a personally useful model. He was temperamentally unequal to the "drunkenness" of his inspired poet. Walt Whitman, of course, was the first fully realized example of the poet-priest as hero, and he is still the greatest. His enlargement of Emerson's vision can be seen best in his preface to the 1855 *Leaves of Grass* and in his heroical essay, *Democratic Vistas*. Whitman's statement of the moral mission of the poet has remained definitive, and some of his twentieth-century successors—Hart Crane and Henry Miller, for instance—have used him as a metaphorical representation of their ideal America or moral Americanism. The sense of prophetic mission has also led some later writers to erupt with Old Testament wrath at the failure of the United States to fulfill its moral potential. It is responsible, for instance, for the raging tone of Patchen's work and the jeremiads of Allen Ginsberg, who is typically Whitmanian in his grandiose belief that he himself represents the regeneration and ultimate triumph of the old ecstatic vision of America.

(3) It is characterized by what Walt Whitman called "personalism." Whitman's term should not be confused with the twentieth-century idealistic philosophy that defines reality as personal and seeks to know the person (that is, God) who perceives and thereby defines the universe. Whitman uses the word inconsistently, but he usually means by it roughly the expression in the individual of the cosmic relationship, the social relationship, and mystical knowledge. That is—and it is his great adjustment of Emersonian individualism—the identity of the person spontaneously and naturally includes communal relationships, the "other," and thus amends the extreme antisocial bias of transcendentalism. It is one proof of Whitman's mystical genius that he recognized, without being limited by, the intensely individual operation of the universal and communal identity discovered in the mystical experience. In practice, the attitude leads Whitman and his successors to celebrate their personalities as expressions of national and universal truth.

Whitman's personalism includes also his attempts to make the book and man one thing, the struggle (as he described it in "A Backward Glance O'er Travel'd Roads") "to articulate and faithfully express in literary or poetic form, and uncompromisingly, my own physical, emotional, moral, intellectual, and aesthetic Personality." The use of literary form to bring the reader into the presence of the artist so that moral imperatives and intimate knowledge may be impressed upon him is one of Whitman's most critically troublesome discoveries. By seeing art as relationship rather than object, it violates much of what at least Western culture has recognized as aesthetic law. The continuity of Whitmanian personalism can be most readily observed in such authors as Henry Miller, in whom autobiography is only thinly disguised, but in one way or another it is a fundamental shaping force for all the writers in Whitman's tradition.

(4) With their commitment to both personalism and heroism, the American literary mystics do not distinguish between art and life. Van Wyck Brooks emphasized this quality when he discussed Whitman's ability to reconcile in his own person intellectual life and the antiintellectualism of the common man.[25] In its literal sense—and American mystics take things literally—the identification of art and life means that the writer is creating himself in literature. By applying this literal usage, we can perhaps engage Malcolm Cowley in an exemplary dialogue about an emendation to the first line of "Song of Myself." Cowley complains that by adding (in 1881) "I sing myself" to the "I celebrate myself" that was the original line, Whitman introduced a theme which "sang" about himself in a narrowly personal way, thereby diluting the theme of universal identity in the first version of the poem.[26] This reading of Whitman's revision is indifferent to the characteristic of mysticism that expresses communal and universal experience in individual personality, as well as to a possible meaning of the words themselves. Rather than "I sing about this worldly self of mine," Whitman's half-line might be better paraphrased as "I create myself by singing." The phrase would thus introduce the theme of the poetic making of life that informs much of Whitman's work. A complementary application of the identification of art and life as Whitman understood it—or as Miller or Merton or Williams understood it[27]—is that one creates a literature first, by living his day-to-day life well.

Perhaps Cowley's disagreement with Whitman illustrates the chief problem in both personalism and the related identification of life and art. Cowley is not really objecting to a Whitman who is insufficiently universal or whose conduct belies his beliefs; he is objecting, rather, to certain elements in Whitman's character that he dislikes. And it is proper for him to do so—as long as he keeps aware of what he is doing. Literature that expresses the personality of the artist depends in part on the reader's willingness to accept the artist on his own terms. The character of the poet as well as his craftsmanship is exposed, and he is thus laying upon himself the tremendous responsibility that to be a good writer he must be a good man. Whitman, Miller, and Patchen have often met resistance from critics because they are difficult individuals. It is, however, a tribute to them as men when their writings stand up under critical scrutiny.

(5) It is commonly distinguished by mystical identification, both with other human beings and with things. This characteristic of many mysticisms often merges with the idea of democratic brotherhood in its American expression. The poet accepts a series of selves through which to write, or writes as that American identity which includes many voices. This one great communal voice, expressed in various individual spokesmen, is the authorial identity of such books as Williams's *In the American Grain* or Whitman's *Drum-Taps*.

The use of mystical identification as a narrative device is also meant to expose the reader, as well as the poet, to a common identity, and to force him to experience the passion and suffering of others—as in the account of the ordeal of the shipwrecked people in section 33 of "Song of Myself," with its sad but triumphant coda: "I am the man, I suffer'd, I was there." Even the comic possibilities of the technique have not been neglected. One might quarrel with Richard Chase's claim that Whitman burlesqued his own style in some of his more outrageous cataloguing of identities,[28] but the tone of Allen Ginsberg's apocalyptic comment on American defensiveness is unmistakable. "I am the defense early warning radar system," he intones in "Death to Van Gogh's Ear," "I see nothing but bombs."

(6) It involves a peculiar view of reality by which the "thing in itself" is seen and valued for its own sake rather than for its meaning. This quality of perception is true of American literary mysticism as a development rather than as a fixed characteristic.

It is only partly true, for instance, of Emerson, who urged his American scholars to recognize the inherent worth of familiar things, but who had a tendency to look at a tree and see an aphorism. Whitman, however, while he still voices the Emersonian doctrine of correspondence and takes natural objects as symbols of spirit, is willing in practice to point to the things and let the meaning go. "The mica on the side of a rock" and the "Fourth-month showers" have "an intricate purpose," but Whitman doesn't bother to articulate it. He assumes, whether consciously or not, that the purpose is named when the thing is named. The same implicit assumption is operating in the catalogs for which he became notorious. Any writer who uses catalogs extensively—Whitman, Williams, Thomas Wolfe, Henry Miller, or Gary Snyder—bets on his ability to create a coherent world simply by naming its objects, what Whitman called the "dumb, beautiful ministers" of reality. In general, this mystical characteristic rises from the assumption that America and its historical uniqueness make possible a new perception, that the awakened citizen of the New World can see things freshly and name them with new names, because the old names and categories no longer apply. The insistence that the thing is its own meaning also reflects the general mystical tendency for symbolism to become absolute.

(7) It is most readily identified by its distaste for traditional form and its insistence on formal freedom. With the possible exception of Hart Crane, all of our literary mystics reject forms and genres that they associate with the past and its failures, and argue that the poem should grow naturally according to its own impulse—"as unerringly and loosely as lilacs or roses on a bush, and take shapes as compact as the shapes of chestnuts and oranges and melons and pears, and shed the perfume impalpable to form," as Walt Whitman said in a famous statement of the organic principle from the preface to the 1855 *Leaves*. Each poem rises mysteriously out of Poetry in much the same way that the individual natural object rises out of Godhead, or Oversoul, or Brahman, or whatever. The imposition, then, of a form (such as a sonnet) that was developed in response to different experience is stifling.

This hostility to tradition has a political and cultural as well as an artistic reference. American mystical writers have, by and large, been cultural revolutionaries, and their defiances of authority have often led them to a kind of philosophical anarchism—Whitman, Thoreau, Miller, and Patchen are examples. Their insistence on naturalness in literary form parallels their insistence on a naturalness in their personal lives which has often been socially unacceptable.

(8) It delights and trusts in sensual and explicitly sexual experience, and has always offended a significant number of conservative readers. The offensiveness may seem a trivial characteristic, but, excepting, for different reasons, the transcendentalists, Van Wyck Brooks, and Thomas Merton, it is remarkably consistent. Whitman was fired from the Department of the Interior and had an edition of the *Leaves* banned in Boston; many of his sexual descriptions still seem unusually earthy and exciting. William Carlos Williams cultivated a certain vulgarity of language and feeling in much of his poetry, and had censorship troubles with his play, *Many Loves*. Thomas Wolfe considered his own sexual descriptions so potentially offensive that he considered making sweeping expurgations in *Look Homeward, Angel*. Kenneth Patchen managed to offend two generations with his erotica and his bluntness, and he played upon one widely held image of himself in *Memoirs of a Shy Pornographer*. Henry Miller, of course, possessed one of the horripilating reputations of the twentieth century.

These writers' directness of sexual description is neither gratuitous nor perverse, nor, with the possible exceptions of Wolfe and John Steinbeck, is it to be explained as realism. Sex is celebrated as a life-force, a natural universal rhythm like that of the sea or the Yin-Yang, and as experience so intense that it approximates the condition of being in itself by gathering all attention into it. It is also prized because of the same tantric impulse that made the Song of Solomon (or Canticles) the favorite scripture of such theoretically asexual Christians as Saint John of the Cross and the Puritans of New England. In Eastern systems, the tantra is the discourse delivered by Shiva (in Buddhism, the bodhisattva) to his Shakti, or female emanation, while in the act of sexual intercourse. It symbolizes the union of intellect and emotion, and of the other complementary opposites of the Yin-Yang. As the definitive metaphor for union with the divine, the sexual image is characteristic of such mystical expressions as Gnostic Christianity and Moslem Sufism, as well as Buddhist and Hindu tantricism and the mystical reading of the Song of Songs. The American variation expresses sexual exaltation more openly in terms of everyday life, and consequently renders it both more offensive and more evasive of conventional moral categories. In this, as in many of its characteristics, American mystical writing is a challenge to preconceptions and a reward for adventurousness. It may be messy or boisterous or wrongheaded, but it is rarely predictable or boring.

Chapter 2

Patchen: A Mystical

Writer's Career

"And Patchen?" she asked, pencil poised.

"Oh, Patchen—nobody takes him seriously," one of them said. "He's just a rough-neck who never grew up."

"He's just a boring child—a lot of noise about nothing," another said.

"Patchen missed the boat," Mr. Brill said. "He made the mistake of thinking a poem was a sort of garbage pail you could throw anything into and a lot of the time he certainly went beyond the pale altogether."

—Patchen, *Memoirs of a Shy Pornographer*

I am no pioneer in my approach to Kenneth Patchen. Nearly all of the critics and reviewers of the work he published for some thirty-five years eased their problems of definition and judgment by calling him a mystic. On the one hand, that body of common opinion validates and encourages my enterprise; on the other, it represents the gravest of critical dangers. Nothing seems more likely to discourage the reader of nonsectarian books about mysticism than the vagueness of reference the concept has attracted, and Patchen has been hurt by it. The attribution of mysticism has been as often derogatory as affirmative, has as often dismissed as identified Patchen's work. It is an example of the loosely metaphorical and invocatory usage about the mystical life that annoyed Thomas Merton, who complained in *The Ascent to Truth*, his study of Saint John of the Cross, that: "Since the Romantic Revival the term mysticism has been usurped by literary critics and historians and applied to anyone who has sought to liberate the emotional and affective life of man from the restraint of conventional or reactionary norms of thought. In fact, any political or artistic dreamer who could bring tears to your eyes or smother you with sensations of unutterable *Weltschmerz* was considered a 'mystic.'"[1]

Merton's own definition of mysticism was, for good reason, rigorously exclusive, and he would have resisted suggestions that he think in mystical terms about Patchen, even though he admired Patchen's work and heard in it echoes of Saint John of the Cross.[2] However, it may be that my predecessors were often right for the wrong reasons, and I may be able to justify their vocabulary, if not always their insightfulness, in part by looking at the shape of Patchen's career. Such an inquiry must rely upon implication and indirection, because Patchen's testimony about mystical experience is lacking. Although he often tantalizes us with hints of personal narrative, they are but sparkles from the wheel. Patchen is never explicitly autobiographical, nor does he write veiled autobiography in any extensive way. Rather, he makes himself known to us according to the qualities of imagination and perception we feel in his writing, which in overview assume a suggestive pattern.

Patchen's literary output falls naturally into three distinct phases, which require the exercise of only modest ingenuity to be compared to the three stages of mystical development identified by patristic Christianity—the sequence of illumination (or conversion), purgation, and union.[3] The traditional theological language may seem incongruous, but, when secularized, the three stages define accurately Patchen's progression as a writer and thinker. His mystical impulse is expressed not in religious terms, but in his idea of the artist, his attitude toward the self, his very diction and syntax. At one level, he develops from the political revolutionary, determined to reform familiar institutions, to the visionary who has seen and re-created a transcendent world with its own geography, laws, and citizenship.

The particular terms of Patchen's development may be represented by the way he regrouped the opening and closing selections in his *Collected Poems* (1968). He had opened his first book, *Before the Brave* (1936), with "when in the course of human events," a poem that invokes egalitarian revolution, pronounces judgment on the past, and announces the new order ("Turn out the lights around the statues. . . . Their time is up. The curtain's down. We take power"). For *Collected Poems*, however, Patchen chose to begin closer to his subsequent thematic interest. The lines that now introduce his life's work are: "Let us have madness openly, O men/ Of my generation." A similar selectivity is at work at the end of *Collected Poems*. The last volume collected is *When We Were Here Together* (1957), which ended with its title poem, a fine cry of anguish against the corrupting influence of society. Patchen replaced it with a short lyric that restates by implication many of his important themes, and is explicitly a celebration of what he called elsewhere "the architecture of our innocence." The *Collected Poems*,[4] then, begins with insanity and ends in triumph in the calm world of a poem which one commentator characterized as "almost saintly":[5]

> Wide, wide in the rose's side
> Sleeps a child without sin,
> And any man who loves in this world
> Stands here on guard over him. (487)

In the first traditional mystical stage the soul glimpses the primordial goal and is converted to the difficult search for the absolute ground of being. The joy of discovery and excited optimism that usually characterize this experience are paralleled in the first period of Patchen's career, when he published *Before the Brave* and *First Will & Testament* (1939), and defined the terms of his revolution. *Before the Brave* can stand among literary expressions of Patchen's mysticism for the dissociation—both of language and emotion—from which he starts. It is an emotionally powerful book with a few fine poems, but the personality and technique of its author are still immature (Patchen was just twenty-five when it was published). Most reviewers, while acknowledging the power and originality of *Before the Brave*, noticed that Patchen's thought was elliptical and his syntax so strained that he was occasionally incomprehensible. Lines like those opening "Prayer to Go to Paradise with the Asses,"[6] with their too-well disguised exploitation of Christian myth:

> Marshal the quaint barren fogbeats in harbors
> left by wings of those whose mansioned lonely
> powers rode a hermit's riderless hurricane
> into
> the dark-fretted eyes of the Golden City   (32)

are clearly ill-suited to a revolutionary audience and out of keeping with the direct social statement about history's defeat or perversion of old idealisms toward which the poem seems to move. Such language attempts (voluntarily or involuntarily) to mate radical themes with visionary perspectives. It tends to break down boundaries rather than make use of categories for analysis.[7] In 1936, Patchen could not unify his transcendent language and his social protest, and he had yet to discover the peculiar voice that is immediately recognizable in his later work.

Still, *Before the Brave* has much to recommend it. At times Patchen defeats his standoff between manner and matter, and breaks into a dense but probing language, which transforms the proletarian theme into an expression of individual and cosmic as well as social process. Those breakthroughs occur most often in single lines, in which Patchen discovers the aphoristic ability that will characterize his subsequent work. But he also occasionally manages a sustained eloquence, as in the only slightly obscure stanza that concludes the book:

> Who were the property of every dunce and prophet,
> Of every gust of wind, of every goutish giant on earth,
> Are come now to claim ourselves and the profit
> Of an ownership which has been our own since birth.
> We are not cool: our hate has made us wise, not clever.
> Beloved, listen, the stirring of life from the grave—
> The heart breaks with the groan and the grind of a lever
> Which lifts a world whose very sun retreats before the
> brave.   (130–31)

Before the Brave is also interesting for its subdued introduction of Patchen's mystical attitudes. Although far from the center of interest, they are strong enough to have encouraged Amos N. Wilder to devote a chapter to Patchen in his *Spiritual Aspects of the New Poetry* (1940), in which he argued that Patchen belonged to a Marxist church militant.[8] That was a standard explanation for the passion of leftist intellectuals then, and, although it certainly could be made pertinent to Patchen, it led Wilder slightly astray. His misemphasis, however, is probably observable only in retrospect, because Patchen's incipient mysticism can be genuinely confusing. When a typical poem introduces "Comrades" to the fiery "Red Woman" with "Kremlin lamps" in her eyes, and the usual proletarian rhetoric is aimed at specific capitalists and German and Italian fascism, it is startling to come across the definitive statement by which "Fields of Earth" is concluded: "our country is the careless star in man" (78). Not only does the image anticipate Patchen's later emphasis on the indwelling divine, but it may not be entirely an overreading to relate the unexpected adjective "careless" to the "nonchalance" of Walt Whitman's exemplary democrats.

Patchen anticipates another subsequent emphasis in his use of insanity in *Before the Brave*. The imperative "Let us have madness openly" calls upon members of his generation to abandon all contemporary standards, so that as psychological and political outcasts they may dare the insanity of searching for love and light in this "slaughtered age." The association of mystical knowledge with what society calls madness is common enough in literary and philosophical thought to be respectable. "We have agreed that sanity consists in sharing the hallucinations of our neighbours," Evelyn Underhill wrote,[9] and Wallace Fowlie explained the authority of the metaphor of insanity in an essay specifically about poetry and mysticism. "Madness," he argued, "become sanity and the way of life in freedom, could therefore be a simplified definition of a state or experience of those who deliberately set themselves off from the world and thus are better able to understand it."[10]

The heterodox Marxism of *Before the Brave* and the orthodox Catholicism which had influenced Patchen's youth were symbolically shed in a story called "Bury Them in God," which was published in the New Directions annual for 1939.[11] Like many contemporaneous intellectuals, Patchen had been disillusioned by the Stalinist purges of the late thirties, and he responded in part by abandoning the search for an external system, even while he continued to think of himself as a revolutionary. He had never really developed the proper socialist personality anyway, and his recognition of the individualism of the moral life was a major step toward his artistic identity. His new distrust of orthodoxies and refusal to subordinate immediate moral problems to "larger issues" were expressed in one of his uncompromising poems of the period:

> *Those smug saints, whether of church or Stalin,*
> *Can get off the back of my people, and stay off.*
> Somebody is supposed to be fighting for somebody ...
> And Lenin is terribly silent, terribly silent and dead.

"The Hangman's Great Hands," from which these angry lines are taken, was published in *First Will & Testament*, the first book in Patchen's mature style. It contained a remarkable range of poems: protest pieces of the kind familiar from *Before the Brave*, but without the obscure, sometimes turgid language of the earlier book; love poems, often of striking originality and delicacy; fantastic narratives and landscapes; brief dadaist dramas; and social satires. In addition, *First Will & Testament* was characterized by a strong comic element, which had been missing in *Before the Brave*. Although Patchen made no attempt to develop an overall thematic unity, his book in general recorded the experience of a universalized "I" who found his only value in a naturally innocent love which broke down the distinction of human identities, and who lived in a world which betrayed such love, often violently. The development of this "I" linked Patchen with the Whitmanian tradition of American mysticism, and established his conversion, as it were, to his own mystical enterprise.

The association of Patchen and Whitman is, I suppose, open to challenge. Perhaps because the comparison had been frequently made[12] and he wished to resist it, Patchen wrote with some hostility about Whitman's gregariousness and messianism. He mentioned Whitman with distaste in "Bury Them in God," and gave him an unflattering walk-on role as Walter Snowbeard Whitman in one of the dadaist dramas of *First Will & Testament*. Later, however, Whitman became a more ambiguous figure. In *The Journal of Albion Moonlight*, for instance, he was used both as a victim of a failure in our emotional life and as an eloquent spokesman against the horrors of war. Like anyone who was truly informed, directly or indirectly, by Whitman's rowdy spirit, Patchen was well anticipated by the master's statement of revolutionary succession: "He most honors my style who learns under it to destroy the teacher."

Patchen's explicit comments aside, the validity of the comparison with Whitman rests largely on the quality of that "I" on which *First Will & Testament* is built. It is much more accommodating and compassionate than the authorial voice of *Before the Brave*; it is not limited by class or economic position, and is able to identify with even those brutalized by the world. The first poem introduces this "I" in language reminiscent of Whitman's:

> I am standing open.
> You must not lower your eyes.
>
> I want them all to know me.
> I want my breath to go over them.
> They should withhold nothing from me.
> I am a respecter of dirt.

Like Whitman's "self," Patchen's "I" is free. It floats, accepting identities and exposing secrets, sharing the torments of flesh and years as well as transfiguring moments of love. Like Whitman's self also, it is able to probe beneath even a placid exterior in order to share pain. "Peter's Diary in Goodentown" is the first of Patchen's remarkable portraits of gentle individuals who live at the threshold between the natural and supernatural worlds and experience the terrors of both.

Patchen's poetic self is also related to Whitman's in its prophetic and visionary function; it is the spokesman for the human spirit and the umpire of the moral life. Whitman's optimism and Patchen's bitter rage originate in the same idealizing vision of America and human capability, and each man assumes at times the point of view that characterizes the other. The potential harshness of judgment Whitman brought to his nation is established in a relatively ignored passage from *Democratic Vistas*. "I say of all this tremendous and dominant play of solely materialistic bearings upon current life in the United States," as Whitman discussed the relationship between material and spiritual progress, "that they must either be confronted and met by at least an equally subtle and tremendous force-infusion for purposes of spiritualization . . . or else our modern civilization, with all its improvements, is in vain, and we are on the road to a destiny, a status, equivalent, in its real world, to that of the fabled damned."[13] Whitman, of course, assumed that the spiritualization would be realized, but many of the twentieth-century writers who have succeeded him have emphasized the consequence of his condition. Patchen, especially, has lived among the fabled damned for all of his adult life, and has recorded their viciousness, smugness, and hypocrisy.

The new mystical attitude is reflected as well in other qualities of *First Will & Testament*. In "The Fox":

> Because she can't afford to die
> Killing the young in her belly
>
> I don't know what to say of a soldier's dying
> Because there are no proportions in death.　　(19)

and in other poems which stress the unity of life, Patchen moves closer to an explicit monism. "The Black Panther and the Little Boy" expresses an almost Buddhistic compassion for the demands of nature, whether gentle or fierce. The tantricism that is to be expected in a poetry stressing unity also surfaces in such poems as "And What with the Blunders," in which sexual lovers leave their physical bodies and journey toward immortality. Finally, Patchen's mysticism begins here to influence his diction, which often becomes paradoxical ("Dying, he turned his face from death") and sometimes names things according to the sounds and meanings of an unfamiliar realm (the Bya Deena of "Peter's Diary in Goodentown"). Language that has significance only if one can assume Patchen's context is relatively unusual in *First Will & Testament*, but becomes important later.

After his conversion to mystical writing, Patchen's career resembles the life of the prototypical mystic even more suggestively. The second period of the traditional mystical way is one of self-torture and near despair. In theological terms purgation is the process by which the old worldly self, the prideful and perverse will, is destroyed in order that the divine or cosmic identity may be apprehended. Psychologically, it is a period of self-mistrust, when one torments himself for his inadequacy before the absolute standard he has sensed and feels irrevocably cut off from the divine. This period in Patchen's career corresponds to the duration of World War II, which becomes in his work the agency of destruction for that suffering humanity which is the identity accepted by the mystical poet.

Patchen introduced the themes of war and the death of the self in *The Journal of Albion Moonlight* (1941), a hallucinatory narrative of pilgrimage. Here he gives his first vigorous expression to what D. H. Lawrence claimed to be the archetypal theme of American literature: the sloughing off of the decadent self which is rooted in history and sin and the emergence of a new self with a new relationship to others.[14] Albion Moonlight, the author-narrator-hero who is explicitly an Everyman, journeys increasingly deeply into the forbidden areas of his own identity, shedding protective layers of self, until a series of deaths that leave the actual act of dying obscure frees him from the perceptual limitations of the human condition, so that he recognizes identity and causality. The war that is the setting for the narrative (the *Journal* is about the "plague summer" of 1940, but the war it describes is all war and is everywhere) represents the failure of history and the alienation of humanity from its own nature. This dissociation (between man and "his animal," as Patchen put it) is one of the many failures of wholeness in the early work. The nature that has been betrayed is the innocence and holiness of perception that Patchen insists is the essential human condition.

Reason has been betrayed too. In this violently deranged book, Patchen continues to use insanity as a key metaphor for mystical insight, and analyzes extensively the relative sanity and insanity of the human community. "There is a new plague," Albion writes near the end of his *Journal*. "There is a plague from which there is no escape for anyone. *The great grey plague*—the plague of universal madness" (305). In the world of the *Journal* consciousness has been so distorted by the institutionalization of everything antithetical to human nature (war, economic competition, hatred) that people have accepted as real the fables of original sin and the fallen world. Behavior according to that misunderstanding is insane, and in a world of total insanity there is no reference for sanity—that is, sanity ("sharing the hallucinations of our neighbors") is itself insane. Only the poet-mystic, who perceives the reality beyond that defined by the defeated institutional consciousness, and who consequently is considered mad by his neighbors, is truly sane. As a social being, Albion is insane because he is forced to think with communal concepts, but as a mystic and visionary, who is capable finally of innocent perception, he achieves absolute sanity. The madness of the world forces him to write a raving book in order to be sane.

The *Journal* reflects another of society's challenges to Patchen the man in its theme of the alienation of the artist from his art. Because artistic forms and language itself are part of the institutionalized insanity against which he struggles, the artist must in a sense abandon art. He must recognize a distinction between human and traditionally artistic values—"as an artist I could have wished that there had been more structure and design to it [the *Journal*]—as a man, that there had been less of the kind there was" (305). Having no art to replace what the world calls "art," but being an artist in need of expression, Albion (or Patchen) resorts to antiart, which uses conventions by inverting or destroying them. The formal pattern of *The Journal of Albion Moonlight*, then, is one of disintegration. The book opens in familiar literary forms (the journal, the romance, the novel) by which we are able to follow the action easily and are kept aware of the relationships within the narrative; but as Albion moves increasingly out of his diseased self the familiar forms break down, and it becomes increasingly difficult to discover what is "really" happening. By the time Albion is free of his old identity, formal categories have collapsed altogether. The *Journal* reads at its ending like a collection of the scraps found in the rubble of an exploded library. In subsequent books the search for an art to replace what he was forced to destroy occupies much of Patchen's attention and becomes one sustained pattern of healing integration.

The Journal of Albion Moonlight was followed by *The Teeth of the Lion* (1942), a small collection of poems notable chiefly for its shrill anger and the hostility of the few reviews it received. *The Dark Kingdom*, also published in 1942, is a superior book, both in literary quality and as an expression of Patchen's mysticism. Here Patchen for the first time attempted to create his own world, with its own laws, according to his own vision. The full title is a page-long prose-poem, which reads in part: "The Dark Kingdom stands above the waters as a sentinel warning man of danger from his own kind. On its altars the deeds of blood are not offered; . . . What has been common and tarnished in these poor wombs, here partakes of immortality. . . . All who have opposed in secret are here provided with green crowns. . . . Here all who sorrow and are weary under strange burdens—fearing death, are seen to enter the white throne room of God." The darkness of the title is, of course, the darkness of Saint John of the Cross's *Dark Night of the Soul*, and Patchen respects the ambiguity of the image. Although his kingdom is a place of great distress and evil, often ragingly violent and animalistic, it is also a place of promise.

Evil in *The Dark Kingdom* provokes Patchen to an almost uncontrollable anger, because it is in a sense absolute. Patchen acknowledges no Emersonian compensation by which evil becomes a subordinate element in a cosmic pattern that is actively working toward good. Emerson, Whitman, even Henry Miller, are perhaps more typical mystics, because they are willing to step momentarily outside human affairs and view the whole with dispassionate imagination—to see that evil is illusory, or that it is that part of human nature still in the process of evolution. But Patchen does not understand evil—that is, he recognizes its existence, but not its necessity. To him, evil is unnatural. Humanity is by nature innocent, kind, loving, full of wonder; evil is a disease caused by human failure to respect that nature. Because Patchen does not accept compensation or related ideas about a compensatory afterlife, he feels that no evil act can ever be redressed. The existence of an original innocent world does not justify the failures of the immediate human world. The impending apocalypse cannot restore what the evils leading to it have destroyed. Evil is simply a violation. Evil must incessantly be resisted.

The Dark Kingdom is not only evil, however. Here, humanity

has descended so far into itself that it is able to face, and perhaps overcome, the ultimate horror. In some of the poems we recognize that Patchen's world is frightening only because it is strange. Many of the weird beings and rituals he invokes are gentle and wonderful, and we misunderstand when we project our secret fears upon them. Although the book is haunted by a tone of preternatural terror, that terror rises from self-knowledge and a purgation of self that can lead the brave spirit to both human and divine fulfillment.

The mysticism of *The Dark Kingdom* is at heart like that of the earlier books. It exploits the same prophetic "I" as *First Will & Testament* and *The Journal of Albion Moonlight*, makes use of the same vantage point of insanity, and celebrates the same tantricism. It differs chiefly in its greater reliance on the special language Patchen first used in *First Will & Testament*. Here we are introduced to people named Ad and Cuu, who live in towns like Lenada, Criha, and Mega, along the Cumber road. In one sense, these are private names for private experience, but in another sense they are part of a remarkably evocative public language which takes its imagery and diction from that racial memory Carl Jung called the collective unconscious. Unlike the prophecies of William Blake, to which it has been compared, *The Dark Kingdom* does not ask the reader to discover an allegorical or anagrammatical significance in its strange terminology. The words are their own meaning, and when we are introduced, for instance, to "Tegos, who is the Bishop/ of Black Church—near Tarn," we should not feel compelled to go rummaging through the scholarship of the various historical Black Churches, but should recognize the indisputable need for an established Black Church in a Dark Kingdom.

After *The Dark Kingdom* Patchen published *Cloth of the Tempest* (1943), a discussion of which can stand for *The Teeth of the Lion* and other books like it from the same period, for example, *An Astonished Eye Looks out of the Air* (1945) and *Pictures of Life and of Death* (1946). These are uneven collections of poems without any deliberate thematic unity, and, although each contains excellent work, they are not particularly good books. In elaborating his themes of cosmic terror and moral outrage, Patchen is often repetitious, his prophetic voice is sometimes nothing more than raw anger, and he is at times liable to the artistic deterioration that had been a thematic concern in *The Journal of Albion Moonlight*. *Cloth of the Tempest*, however, includes in its philosophical poems about Confucius, Lao Tzu, Mohammed, and Buddha the first expressions of Patchen's interest in Eastern mysticisms. These poems display considerable familiarity with Eastern philosophies and are directed sympathetically at central philosophical problems. "Lao Tsze," for instance, considers the troublesome Taoist attitude that regards attempts to share enlightenment as weak or foolish.

Cloth of the Tempest also developed the visual element in the integration of mysticism and art that Patchen had first used in *The Journal of Albion Moonlight*. In these early books it is rarely anything more than inspired doodling, but it becomes fundamental in later years. Although *Cloth of the Tempest* contains a number of rather complex visual compositions, its pictorial element generally takes the form of crude stick figures, and at its best it contributes to an epigrammatic wit—as in the poem which consists of concentric squares, surrounded by footprints, and enclosing the text: "The Impatient/ Explorer/ invents/ a box in which/ all journeys/ may be kept." Many of the poems in these books are also typographically experimental. Patchen's inventiveness may be demonstrated by his discovery (or at least anticipation) here of the concrete poetry which would become an important mode more than a decade later.[15]

Patchen continued to integrate verbal and visual effects in *Panels for the Walls of Heaven* and *Sleepers Awake* (both 1946). *Sleepers Awake* is a long, typographically eccentric prose narrative, which extends many of the concerns of *The Journal of Albion Moonlight*, but with even less of a sustained story. Although more uneven than *Sleepers Awake*, *Panels for the Walls of Heaven* culminates the second, or purgative, stage of Patchen's career, and consequently is more interesting for immediate purposes. Its forty-four panels are either verbal or visual (or, infrequently, both) expressions of extreme rage, frustration, and fear. They range in quality from some of Patchen's most successful single pieces to expressionistic outbursts which are at best inarticulate, and which may represent the final appearance of the artist as inspired madman.

The terror and despair of this strange book are all but unrelieved. Opening with a lament for a lost clean world, it moves to a final rejection of hope and an invitation to death. While Patchen continues to recommend his old remedies, love and art are powerless here as they had never been previously. Love is simply a moment's escape from terror; art is an almost gratuitous bleat against the apocalyptic thunder. Overwhelmingly, *Panels for the Walls of Heaven* is about the triumph of death, both individual and collective, and in death is found neither hope nor rest. Death is rather the fundamental terror, and its characteristic description is as a sickening, involuntary removal to a nightmarish country, a ground of blood and filth. One almost inevitably sees in *Panels for the Walls of Heaven* a correspondence to the despair and loss of personal will which in mystical autobiography precedes illumination. It is Patchen's most unrelievedly grim and humorless book.

The point of transition to the unitive third phase is difficult to locate because of the cluster of books Patchen published in 1945 and 1946. His state of mind, and consequently the tone of his work, was unsettled during these years of psychological reaction and counterreaction, when he shifted back and forth between bleak pessimism and geniality.[16] A relaxed hilarity not found in his earlier humor informs his prose romance, *Memoirs of a Shy Pornographer* (1945), which was published before several of the titles I have assigned to the second period. The structure of *Memoirs* can be analyzed according to an influential model of the mystical way and for the first time Patchen permits himself something resembling a traditional happy ending—in a comic-strip heaven, which is made up largely of primitivistic and alchemical paintings, and which represents the power of the artistic imagination to create its own salvation. As an ultimate goal, however, the afterlife of *Memoirs* is too significantly fictive. That another world is needed to enjoy a normal family life with all of its jealous squabbles—which is what the heaven of *Memoirs* provides—is clearly a radical irony in Patchen's thoughts about salvation.

However the ambiguities of *Memoirs* are finally to be interpreted, the pessimism of Patchen's early career is distinctly eased with the publication in 1946 of *They Keep Riding Down All the Time*, a short prose narrative set in a house by the sea, where the protagonist and his lover are admittedly "leading impossible lives in an impossible world." Although Patchen has not abandoned moral indignation, the tone of this little book is calm, reflective—wise, one is tempted to say. Its imperturbability is explained by the title sentence: "O they keep riding down all the time. Nobody can ever stop them. Some from the light and some from the darkness—O see with what stern tenderness they keep riding down on this world!" (13). The "they" of the passage is not particularly paraphrasable, but refers to something like "the messengers of death," and the emphasis on time and motion in the title indicates that Patchen has come to understand death as process rather than the ugly end of process it had been earlier. His description of the organic universe of mysticism helps to justify his sense of resolution and confidence:

> Sometimes I think that every man's life has a meaning in a greater life which is being lived by a single creature whose nerves and cells and tissues we are. Just as there is no star, but stars; no tree, but trees; no brook or hill or sea which exists alone from all others of its kind; no road, but roads whose direction is everywhere; just as there is no pain or joy or fear which has not been felt by all of us; so must there forever be no man, but men whose lives cross and recross in a majestic pattern, unknowing, unstained, and beautiful, therefore, beyond comprehension. We are, to put it another way, cells in the brain of God. (17)

The theme of fulfillment even in the teeth of destruction is simplified in *See You in the Morning* (1947), the story of two lovers whose faith overcomes the emotional weight of war and death. *See You in the Morning* was Patchen's only novel and his only compromise with the marketplace. He wrote it in the best imitation of a popular style he could muster in an attempt to recover for his publisher some of the large sums that had been lost in the publication of *Sleepers Awake*.[17] It is embarrassingly sentimental, and its traces of the mystical theme are left undeveloped.

Patchen returned to his serious work in *Red Wine & Yellow Hair*

(1949), a collection of poems in which quiet wisdom continues to control the rage of the early work. Although still preoccupied with death, horror, and failure, Patchen no longer seems personally threatened by them, and he is frequently as whimsical as he is bitter. He writes now with compassion rather than anxiety about human suffering, and his ability to share pain fulfills one condition of the Whitmanian technique he developed in *First Will & Testament*. The triumphs of *Red Wine & Yellow Hair* are the compassionate portraits—"The Lute in the Attic," "A Plate of Steaming Fish," "Old Man," and "Poor Gorrel"—in which the humanity of even the crooked, failed, and ugly is made accessible and celebrated.

Orchards, Thrones & Caravans, a collection later incorporated into *When We Were Here Together*, was published in 1952, and *Fables and Other Little Tales*, the first of Patchen's books to be written wholly out of the special culture of union, appeared the following year. *Fables* can best be described as a series of anecdotes about people who live in a genial version of the Dark Kingdom. Its chief forms are variations on the allegorical story (Patchen's allegories often seem exact, but elude paraphrase) and the explanatory animal fable, complete with moral application. Patchen's explanations are always thorough in this very fabulous book, and they often become exercises in extending his outrageous ingenuity beyond decent limits—as in "The Evolution of the Hippopotamus," which involves a horse, a bathing suit, and a swimming race, among other improbable details.

Like the later *Because It Is* (1960), which differs chiefly by being written in verse, and for which the present discussion can stand, *Fables* has often been compared to the nonsense of Edward Lear. The comparison is apt, although Lear's reputation as a children's writer may be misleading. Children might enjoy many of these *Fables* because their unstated theme has to do with the joys of discovery and the virtues of play, and certainly we must recover at least something of the imaginative world of childhood to read them to our own profit. But in another sense, Patchen's work is not for children at all. In spite of his high spirits, he exposes greed and brutality in his humorous world, and frequently he drops into a sudden spasm of pain. It would be foolhardy to attempt to paraphrase the book, but the first and last fables—the first with its poignant metaphors of process, and the last with its mythological models of both celebration and destiny—appear to introduce and complete a body of thematically related work. The themes are youth and age, love, birth and death, and change.

More pertinent to our concern with the unitive state, *Fables* and *Because It Is* are written in the special language for which Patchen had been building the vocabulary since *First Will & Testament*. It is the spiritual creole of a far country where the usual categories have been defeated and things as well as sentient creatures share a common life. Like the languages of all mysticisms it is heavily paradoxical, and it is more particularly Patchen's in its punning and its slippery allusiveness. Patchen incessantly uses cliches, but always twists them in order to salvage some significance. "Tat for Two," "The Business, as Usual," and "Because Sometimes the Handwriting Eats Away the Wall" are titles that exploit the garbled cliche or allusion in obvious ways. More often, we are tantalized, but not satisfied, by the apparent familiarity of a phrase to which Patchen has refused to return the old meaning. The closeness of his language to English permits us to share the landscape of his imagination, but his slight strangeness of syntax and his portman-teau vocabulary keep us from lapsing into our native tongue. In this way Patchen eases the tension that troubled his experiments with integral language in *The Dark Kingdom*, where the strange vocabulary often became intrusive by appearing to invite transla-tion into some traditional allegory.

Something of the formal experimentation of *Fables* (which one notice helplessly labeled "semi-prose") was continued in *The Famous Boating Party and Other Poems in Prose* (1954), notable chiefly for a few good poems in a genre which Patchen had earlier used only rarely and with indifferent success. He attained a more significant stage in his development in 1955–56 with the publica-tion of *Glory Never Guesses* and *A Surprise for the Bagpipe Player*, two packets of silk-screened "poem-paintings" which he later collected in a limited edition entitled *The Moment* (1960). These large, bright, inventive artifacts fully integrate into his poetry the visual element of such earlier books as *Cloth of the Tempest* and *Sleepers Awake*. Patchen's marriage of painter and poet had also been expressed in his series of "painted books," in which he decorated the boards by hand. Such efforts had only limited success; visual artistry never became integrally related to the text. The silk-screened poems, however, merged the two ways of art fully into one another. The poem is not broken into lines or stanzas, but takes its shape from the space of the painting, and usually is organically part of the picture. In the best of the silk screens, the visual element, paradoxically oblique language, and epigrammatic wit combine to produce a tersely suggestive work of art—as in a composition of red and white rectangles, arranged so as to give the illusion of great perspective, in which the text— "With one tiny stick/ To arrange the air over the eating-shed/ And the evil part of the earth around it/ So that at last/ Not even the stick is left"—is set at varying distances into the geometrical structure.[18]

In 1957 Patchen published his first collection of miscellaneous verse since 1949, *When We Were Here Together*, and *Hurrah for Anything*, a book of illustrated comic poems in a form related to the limerick. *When We Were Here Together* also includes comic poems, as well as contemporary nursery rhymes, love lyrics, poems of horror and protest, mythologies, and psychological portraits. Many of these poems are written in a new form based on word and line count, which Frederick Eckman considered clearly a "sonnet variation."[19] Whether or not Eckman was correct, Patchen's ability to use this tight form for extremes of expression is impressive, as is a similar dexterity in *Hurrah for Anything*, and in general all of his formal experimentation during the 1950s.

After *Hurrah for Anything*, Patchen brought out *Poemscapes* (1958), another book in a new form: page-long prose-poems, with regular spatial divisions within them. The formal discoveries of this book continue the patterns of integration after 1946, but the speaker of *Poemscapes* is more immediately striking than its form. Whoever he is, he is wise and free, like some absurdist Montaigne, and he has gained a perspective by which he understands both the world's rhythms and conflicts. He is the transcendent Whitmanian poet-hero, turning his world over on his page, naming its realities, creating its values. Although he shares the anger about injustice and hypocrisy that marked the career of Kenneth

Patchen, he is beyond the power of such things to hurt him. He answers, finally, the request Patchen had made in his first book, more than twenty years before:

> O give us words that shrug
> Giant shoulders at the false display of poetry
> That does not show the pilgrim far before the
> brave. (25)

Patchen next turned his hand to playwriting. *Don't Look Now* was produced in Palo Alto in 1959 and off Broadway a few years later (as *Now You See It*). *Because It Is* followed in 1960, and after it Patchen did not publish another book until *Hallelujah Anyway* and *But Even So* in 1966 and 1968 respectively. Both were collections of the poem-paintings which had become increasingly less accessible to literary analysis, and, with the passing of time, more steeped in calm wisdom. Patchen had never been very much at home in the world, and he seemed to grow cheerful and confident as he prepared to leave it. Although he was a semiinvalid during these years, his work showed no diminution of the feistiness of the old days ("This room, this battlefield" is the motto of one of the poems in *But Even So*), but it does show a kind of exemplary mystical nonattachment, a refusal to define oneself according to the results of battle, even while continuing to fight lustily.

In these books also the poetic and visual lines have become inseparably integrated. The arrangement of words is balanced in the area between space and grammar, and the strange protoplasmic figures with which Patchen peoples his visionary world create an emptiness around them which is nicely filled by his calligraphy. In the portentous context established by the mixed form, Patchen's talent for epigrammatic wit and syntactical balance is particularly fortunate. A lifetime of emotional, technical, and thematic concern is gathered into the best of these picture-poems—in, for instance, a compact text from *Hallelujah Anyway*: "Man is not/ a/ town/ where things/ live/ but a/ worry &/ a weeping/ of unused wings."

As a vehicle by which Patchen coordinated his creative energies, the poem-painting identifies one culmination of his career and one of the resolutions he reached for his personal perturbations. His rediscovery of the lore and suggestiveness of mysticism coincided with his creation of new forms of perception, and so he returns us to the timelessness of art and its sources in human experience.

Chapter 3

Personalism

This hour I tell things in confidence,
I might not tell everybody but I will tell you.
    —Whitman, "Song of Myself"

You have read many books. This book is reading you.
    —Patchen, *The Journal of Albion Moonlight*

"Patchen," Leo Kennedy wrote in a review of *Cloth of the Tempest*, "is a thoroughly irritating young man who endeavors to shock with effrontery where he cannot impress with talent." Reviewing the same book for *The Nation*, H. P. Lazarus reached similar conclusions: "Patchen is not a serious poet. And his fulsome self-indulgence combined with the continual intrusion of a personality that insists on talking, singing, weeping, fighting, and cooing to itself, is very trying."[1] Kennedy and Lazarus may or may not have known that they were responding to one of the techniques of self-expression characteristic of the mystical literary tradition of Walt Whitman and were paying a sort of left-handed tribute to the personalism through which the potentialities of mystical identity find specific expression.

Patchen made no attempt to defend himself against these critical dismissals. In fact, he was so gratified by their wrath that he borrowed them as blurbs for the dust jacket of the second edition. The gesture is typical of the pleasure Patchen, Henry Miller, Allen Ginsberg, and other mystical writers take in their personal offensiveness to the decorum of what they regard as official literary society. Their enthusiasm for the obscene or outrageous gesture may seem merely childish, and at times it is indeed generically related to the youthful discovery of the fart in church, but it also expresses a sense of personal force, a profound rebelliousness, and a celebration of freedom. Leslie Fiedler, introducing Whitman to a general audience, felt that his success depended on making him "come to seem again as offensive as he really is."[2] The association of personal, ethical, even spiritual power with the power to offend is a side effect of personalism, and without much inherent significance. But it does illustrate the degree to which mystical writers cultivate personality as a stance against the world.

Walt Whitman named personalism in a *Galaxy* magazine article of 1868 that he later incorporated into *Democratic Vistas*. Characteristically, he evolved no rigid philosophical guide for behavior from his concept, nor did he define the term with any particular precision. In fact, he used it in what appear to be contradictory ways. *Democratic Vistas* is really a collection of more or less assimilated scraps of published and unpublished articles, journal entries, and other memoranda, and one has to read it with a certain architechtonic creativity of one's own. It would certainly be possible to mine it for more than one interpretation of its thrust and argument. However, by his terminology Whitman seemed to have in mind a loosely defined cluster of interdependent attitudes. By personalism he meant roughly, first, the embodiment in the individual of cosmic potential, or, in other words, the way in which a particular mystic enacts universal law by expressing his particular personality. That process of returning cosmic illumination to the flesh is the Whitmanian version of the unitive life, and is clearly related to both the "deification" of Christian mysticism and the infusion of the universal into the individual described by Eastern adepts.

By thus personalizing the eternal and ineffable, Whitman reasserts the old paradox that the knowledge of the self is the knowledge of the mystical All, and that the recognition of the basis of identity is thus the ultimate sharing of identity and the basis of true community. Whitman recognizes no unqualified "I"; his concept of the person assumes a necessary, spontaneous element of the not-me.[3] He distinguishes personalism from individualism, which "isolates" (381),[4] and which "continually enlarging, usurping all, [may] seriously affect, perhaps keep down entirely, in America, the like of the ancient virtue of Patriotism" (373). Personalism is rather associated with "adhesiveness or love, that fuses, ties and aggregates, making the races comrades, and fraternizing all" (381). It has a strong utopian component. By making that radical distinction, Whitman recognized and defeated the egocentricity and extreme antisocial bias of Emersonian transcendentalism, and thus avoided the selfishness and privacy that often characterized Emerson's and Thoreau's practice of self-reliance.

In defining personalism in opposition to individualism, Whitman was perhaps applying, consciously or not, some dimly perceived ideas about the Hegelian dialectic of self-definition that were discussed by intellectuals in the United States during the 1840s and 1850s, and hinted at darkly in handbooks and other popularizations of German philosophy.[5] Whitman could, for instance, have derived his idea of personality from the American Hegelian Frederick A. Rauch, whose *Psychology; or, A View of the Human Soul* (1840) was not only the first American book to use the term psychology in its title, but also, as Rauch claimed, "the first attempt to unite *German* and *American* mental philosophy."[6] "The animal," Rauch wrote, "is an individual, that feels itself, but cannot be a person, because it is not conscious of itself. . . . We have [individuality] in common with the animal, while we share personality with the Deity" (175). Rauch's person was the only being who was entitled to speech or through whom the genius of humanity could be spoken.

Further, personality was expansive and generalized. In connection with Whitman, Rauch's elaboration of that principle is instructive:

> Thus in our personality, the general and individual are so united, that the one is contained in the other. This will appear from the following remarks:—We speak of a national spirit, of national honor, of national art and literature; these do not and cannot exist in the abstract, their existence must be concrete. It becomes concrete when the general and individual grow together, . . . when therefore, the general becomes conscious of itself in the individual. Greece, as such, could not become conscious of its honor or literature, but when this general national spirit becomes individualized in a

Plato or Sophocles, it becomes conscious of itself. Hence it is their personality, in which the Greek spirit must center, and through which as its organ, it expresses itself by works of literature and art. True genius, must therefore always bear the character of a national generality . . . and the less individuality appears in its productions, the more valuable it is." (178)

And finally: "Our personality is complete only when we are conscious of God and our relation to him, and when we suffer God to speak to it and through it. . . . Personality is, therefore, that transparent center in man, through which every general and noble activity is to pass, and in which it is to become conscious" (178–79).

I know of no hard evidence that would put Rauch's book into Whitman's hands during those days of the late forties and early fifties when he was tuning his instrument, although it is difficult to imagine that a reader of Whitman's curiosity, taste, and energy could have remained entirely unaware of it. Beyond such biographical speculation, the example of Rauch demonstrates that the intellectual distinction between the individual and the person was current during Whitman's formative period, as was applied (although not original) Hegelianism, and that *Democratic Vistas* can be read in part as a document that takes a position against Emersonian transcendentalism in the controversial literature of transcendental and idealistic philosophies.

We do well, however, to keep in mind that Whitman's priorities were pragmatic, not systematic, and that his paradoxical resolution of communality and individuality in personalism was only incidentally philosophical. Its immediate purpose had to do with healing some of the serious rifts in democratic society. He made no further use of the term personalism after he invented it in *Democratic Vistas*, and he used it there chiefly as a metaphor for a complex of attitudes that informed his poetic program from the beginning. By 1860 he had already been using personality as a concept and calling attention to it with typographical elaborations,[7] and he had implicitly defined the fundamental processes of personalism in several poems of the 1855 *Leaves of Grass*.

In "There Was a Child Went Forth," for instance, Whitman

hints at the nature of personalistic development by the progression of the child's consciousness. Identity is here accumulated by a reciprocal activity of becoming objects perceived and drawing them into the self. Beginning with simple perceptions of natural objects, the child moves into an increasingly complex identification with family and the larger society until his sensual journey brings him to contemplation of the sea. Here the sea does not represent the loss of identity or absorption into a larger identity that might be anticipated in mystical and romantic poems. While it unquestionably suggests expansion of consciousness and a knowledge more than merely human, the child does not become part of it. Rather it becomes part of him, and with it he "now goes and will go forth every day." Elsewhere in the 1855 *Leaves* Whitman summarizes the process thus: "And these one and all tend inward to me, and I tend outward to them,/ And such as it is to be of these more or less I am." This rudimentary personalism not only energizes Whitman; it establishes the shape and character of one typical American experience—the experience, however simplified, of Henry Miller, or the experience of Thomas Wolfe, whose work is in ways little more than an extended commentary on "There Was a Child Went Forth."

In theory the personalist is simply the average but enlightened citizen of spiritualized democracy. In literary practice, however, the idea of personal force in the heroic poet-priest is so strong that he becomes almost exclusively the important exponent of personalism. Despite a tendency to antiintellectualism, American mystical writers identify the one who knows with the one who has the language to express knowledge gracefully. "The man is only half himself," Emerson asserted; "the other half is his expression." In this case Whitman agreed: "Speech is the twin of my vision." The intuitive apprehension of unity is thus indistinguishable from the ability to find some literary analogue for it, and distinctions between art and life are eradicated. In a sense, the poet must create the unitive life and his reader's access to it, even as he lives it.

Personalism, then, especially in the work of a Whitman, a Miller, or a Patchen, is concerned as much with the moral as with the perceptual and existential. Because the poet is hero and priest, his great function is to apply the wisdom he derives from his intuition of mystery to guidelines for a common personal and political life. Just as he himself must respect some ultimate morality in order to be truly a poet, so he is obliged to consider the moral imperative before any other—including the aesthetic—in his poetry. Whitman's moralism differs from the familiar cautionary literature which calls itself moral because rather than appeal to a ready body of emotion or legalistic precedent it defines morality only according to its organic function in a particular situation. In other words, Whitman's moral statement does not exist prior to his personal recognition of the absolute basis for morality; it is inseparable from his presence in his work. Personalism demands of literature a means by which the poet can make his appeal to the reader in person and "tell things in confidence." Not only is the poet both creator and touchstone of the moral life, he is present in his poem to answer for what it says. The poet of personalism cannot indulge in art for its own sake. "Camerado, this is no book," is Whitman's famous dictum; "Who touches this touches a man."

Such attitudes contradict many familiar assumptions about the nature of art. Rather than create an object possessing certain qualities of beauty, harmony, and emotional peace, personalistic writers attempt to create by art a person, replete with the eccentricities, inconsistencies, and needs for expression that distinguish the human personality. In particular, the concept of artistic distance—that the creator must remain removed from the emotion of his work so that he does not intrude upon its balance—is often aggressively violated by these writers. What many of their contemporaries condemn as loss of control, they themselves respect as their need to be heard. The lack of concern with distance in literary personalism, and with it a general distaste for structural irony, marks more than a theoretical difference with formalists and classicists. It can lead to confusion about personalistic work, as it did in Edmund Wilson's now famous misreading of Henry Miller's *Tropic of Cancer*. Repelled by Miller's scabrous account of his life in Paris, Wilson assumed that the narrative voice was unreliable and read the book as an ironic fiction in which the narrator represented the decadence of the American expatriate community. Wilson's explication was scarcely as insensitive as many years later it seems in synopsis. He simply did not recognize Miller's relatively unfamiliar literary tradition, which made no use of the conventions of the modern impressionistic novel; he did not know what Miller later told him in a rejoinder—that "I am the hero, and the book is myself."[8]

Kenneth Patchen's personalism differs from that of Henry Miller or Thomas Wolfe or Whitman himself; it is perhaps closer to that of William Carlos Williams's *Paterson*. Personalism is not important to him as autobiography or the philosophy of the specific individual, but after *Before the Brave* he devotes his resources to breaking down the distance of both artist and reader from the poem in order that his moral statement might find direct voice. That voice does not always belong to the particular Kenneth Patchen who was raised in Ohio, lived in New York, and spent much of his adult life in pain, but it is the voice of the poetic and representative Kenneth Patchen. His positive characters are his spokesmen; he does not distinguish himself from them; they are the persons who bring his moral concerns to the attention of the reader.

Patchen's use of this moralistic literary personalism is seen best, even if with some difficulty, in *The Journal of Albion Moonlight*, in which the nature of moral consciousness and the release of its literary voice are central themes. Here Patchen (or, more exactly, his representative, Albion) repeatedly describes his method in explicitly personalistic terms. "My purpose?" he writes, "It is nothing remarkable: I wish to speak to you."[9] He elaborates this attitude in language that resembles his friend and colleague, Henry Miller's: "Men were made to talk to one another. You can't understand that. But I tell you that the writing of the future will be just this kind of writing—one man trying to tell another man of the events in *his own heart*. Writing will become speech" (200). He emphasizes the intensity of his efforts to make direct contact: "I think you will agree that I am alive in every part of this book; turn back twenty, thirty, one hundred pages—*I am back there*. That is why I hate the story; characters are not snakes that they can shed their skins on every page—there can be only one action: what a man is . . . ah! but I am in the room with you. I write this book *as an action*. Like knocking a man down" (261).

The Journal of Albion Moonlight opens with a series of entries by Albion, who is leading a band of pilgrims toward Galen, the home of Roivas (go ahead, read it it backward), and presumably a place of peace and fulfillment. Although the pilgrims have in a sense abandoned a civilization committed to war and subjected themselves to a nightmarish journey through madness in order to find some better world, they insist that they are not running away. Their pilgrimage is also a missionary venture into America, a last desperate attempt to reestablish innocence—"It was essential that we bring our message to the people who had lost hope in the world. . . . Our religion was life. Flowers, brooks, trees. . . . Now we are held here and the world will perish because no one is saying we love you, we believe in you" (17). The Albion of this early pilgrimage is a defensively tough character who is nevertheless determined to save humanity and is already making his first assaults on the literary culture he associates with the general failure of civilization. His circumstances reflect the plight of the transcendental artist: his journal is written in the service of humanity, but he is threatened with destruction by those who do not understand it.

In these opening pages Albion is also a visionary mystic who is capable from time to time of exultation in a "love for all beings." He experiences mystical identification with other persons, and even participates momentarily in a rapt union with the knowledge and nature of God. However, he is not entirely in control of his mystical faculty, so that the quality of his extensions of self is determined primarily by the nature of the being with which he identifies. Mystical identity depends heavily on perception, and at this point Albion's perception is largely conditioned by the terrifying forces of war and insanity.

Albion's early writing is as largely uncontrolled as his life itself. The journal in which this fragment of the story is told is, of course, a nonliterary mode; it is not given form by an intellect outside of its time and aware of overall causality, but simply follows day-to-day action indiscriminately. The significance of this choice of genres may be explained by Van Wyck Brooks, who for several years early in his career was preoccupied with the moral and spiritual dilemma posed by literary form. Brooks defined poetry in Emersonian terms as the primordial language of spirit ("For poetry was all written before time was," Emerson said). Form, Brooks thought, was a social institution that allowed people to communicate, but was subject to economic and political pressures, and thus stifled in rhetoric the primordial and spontaneous element of poetry. To put poetry into form, then, compromised poetry. The writer must incessantly struggle, to greater or lesser success, with that necessary compromise, but some advanced spirits—Brooks called them sufferers from the "malady of the ideal"—found themselves unable to make it:

> A great vision shatters them. They become fragmentary. They can express themselves only in the intimacy of personal confessions, unrelated, of which every sentence is warm, molten, malleable, without the alloy of rhetoric which gives form and currency to literary works. . . . In their hands the journal becomes a kind of vicarious work of art—the work of art perhaps of souls in harmony with the universal. It endeavors to record the soul's impressions immediately without the brokerage of form, to give an expression to intuitions having the spontaneity of the intuitions themselves.[10]

Brooks was referring specifically to several French journal-keepers, but his observation might illuminate as well the fondness of American mystical writers for the journal form and fictional adaptations of it. Notable examples include the voluminous journals and diaries of Emerson and Thoreau, Whitman's *Memoranda During the War*, Williams's *Kora in Hell* and "The Descent of Winter," Merton's fictional *My Argument with the Gestapo* and autobiographical *The Sign of Jonas*, and Steinbeck's *Log* from *Sea of Cortez*.

Late in his narrative, Albion Moonlight himself becomes a theoretician of the significance of the journal. The passage also defines his symbolic stature:

> The journal, whether real or imaginary, must conform to only one law: it must be at any given moment what the journal-keeper wants it to be at any given moment. It is easily

seen from this that time is of the greatest importance in the journal; indeed, there must be as many journals as there are days covered. The true journal can have no plan for the simple reason that no man can plan his days. Do you seriously doubt this? I did. I ventured forth early this summer with a definite project in my mind: it was my intention to set down the story of what happened to myself and to a little group of my friends—and I soon discovered that what was happening to us was happening to everyone. . . .

It was too late to write a book; it was my duty to write all books. I could not write about a few people; it was my role to write about everyone. (305–6)

The journal, then, records the daily circumstances of the pilgrims, and if the causality of their strange world is sometimes lacking (because Albion only partly understands it), the narrative is relatively uncomplicated and easily followed. It is the movement in time from one place to another toward Galen and Roivas, which are ostensibly positive although vague goals, and the demonic presences that haunt the expressionistic landscape represent the difficulties of the way. After fifty-seven pages, however, Albion begins a novel, the text of which alternates with the journal for nearly the remainder of the book and complicates matters considerably. The novel attempts to understand the events of the journal by fictionalizing them, and its themes, characters, and action are interwoven so tightly with those of the journal that it is impossible to distinguish between them with perfect clarity. Journal and novel, however, are parallel texts, and the particular concerns of the novel are epitomized in the pleadings of a wise hag whom Albion encounters during one of his mystical seizures of self: "I ask ye not to do murder, not to think evil, not to violate the girl-child in the thicket of thy despair" (113). The thematic concern with the violation of the girl-child in the novel parallels the concern with war, the historical obscenity, in the journal. The journal laments the general failure of mankind to find love and peace; the novel records the failure of the individual to respect innocence. In the novel, the meaning of the journey to Roivas (who assumes here overtones of evil) is echoed in the chase after

Leah, Roivas's disturbingly beautiful daughter, whose many in-carnations represent the idealization of the feminine principle, and whose appearances are marked by violent changes of tone. As a transcendental poet, Albion wants desperately to be able to portray tenderness and purity in both woman and the sexual relationship, but he is forced to record instead the details of an essentially sordid struggle for sexual priority. Passages shift within a sentence or so from lyrical delicacy to cynical lewdness, and Albion himself is transformed in as short a space from lover to rapist and murderer.

The violence of the novel is every bit as pervasive as that of the journal, and even more feverish. One nightmarish scene is defini-tive and recurs with compulsive regularity. In it, Albion hurriedly writes his fiction as he is on trial or about to be executed for a rape-murder which he both did and did not commit, which both did and did not happen. Albion is guilty of the crime because he shares as a man in all human guilt, but his judges (usually the other pilgrims) are not swayed by considerations of justice. They are determined to assassinate him solely because, as a poet, he sees through hypocrisy and deceit, and thus represents the destruction of the old world.

The narrative line of *The Journal of Albion Moonlight* breaks into more novels, journals, and abortive scraps of other forms than I have identified here, and it is of some importance to distinguish among them if the fiction is finally to make sense.[11] For our limited purposes, however, the original novel and journal will suffice, because the other formal digressions are basically elabora-tions upon them. The original journal, which runs from 2 May to 27 August, continues throughout the book, although it appears several times to have been abandoned and especially near the end is difficult to follow. The novel supplements the journal nearly to the conclusion of the narrative. In the journal the pilgrimage to Galen progresses (without any consistent geographical orienta-tion) across America, and the American continent becomes the great battlefield of the war. The account of the pilgrimage also develops into an extended satire (interposed with descriptions of war, and lighter in tone) on the American scene. In a series of brief satirical sketches of small-town life in the United States, the pil-grims visit the likes of Buford, Mississippi; Decatur, Illinois; and Saginaw, Michigan.

As Albion grows accustomed to the dangers of the road, his mysticism becomes increasingly less determined by external forces and his literary inspiration increasingly dominant. Among the values metaphorically associated with Galen are absolute identity and true art, and Albion, closing in, becomes powerful enough to change the nature of even the reality he must survive. As the journey nears Galen, and Albion himself is more forcefully offered as the definitive basis of art, the texture of the narrative degenerates, and the journal and novel entries become increasingly difficult to pick out of the literary rubble which clutters every page. Albion's novel, a literary form, simply runs down and collapses into its component parts. The journal, as a nonliterary form, continues to the end. Both novel and journal, however, culminate in a death scene in which the worldly Albion, who shared in the guilt for the girl-child, is destroyed in order that his spiritual self may be released (250), and the narrative ends in a still ambiguous Galen, where Albion again displays the wisdom gleaned from his physical death. That his knowledge is neither comforting nor redeeming indicates the depth of Patchen's despondency during World War II.

Although it is the most reliable narrative element, the movement in time and space from the New York of 2 May to the Galen of 27 August provides no indisputable reality on which to build an interpretation. Near the end, a parallel entry for 2 May in "The Little Journal of Albion Moonlight" (there has been one other variant entry for this first day of the pilgrimage) suddenly informs us that Albion has never left home. "There is more of the world here in this room with me than I can understand" (306), he tells the friends who would have been (and in the main narrative are) his companions on the way. The surprise is not meant to confuse or complicate the story line, but to return the fiction to its definitive vision of what is real—the author at his desk.

The Journal of Albion Moonlight is about itself, its growth, and its own authorial narrative consciousness. It systematically destroys the conventional responses readers bring to fiction in order that Albion Moonlight (who is simply the poetic aspect of Kenneth Patchen) may expose the reader to his moral perception without the intermediary stages of meaning fiction usually employs. His attacks on traditional literary form are meant to explode the audience-consciousness that distinguishes books from other realities and force us to accept him, rather than our usual authorities, as our guide. His role as Whitmanian poet-priest informs two character-istic passages from *The Journal*: "The great writer will take a heroic stand against literature: *by changing the nature of what is to be done*, he will be the first to do what the voice of dreaming does; he will heal the hurt where God's hand pressed too hard in His zeal to make us more than the animals" (308); and: "Thus, against murder, against hypocrisy, and for life, for all that is most beauti-ful and noble in man, for the immense joy of being alive, do I speak. I am an island in a cess-pool called History" (204). This purpose challenges the writer to create a new body of literary assumptions, which Patchen attempts to incorporate into the figure of Albion himself.

Albion Moonlight is the author of his various narratives at the same time that he is a character in them, and he is openly aware that he is a created literary character in a fiction (although both "character" and "fiction" are in a process of redefinition). Be-cause he is his own creator, and because of a perverse convention he adopts for his narrative—"this novel is being written as it happens" (145)—he must continue writing to continue living; it is only through art that he can overcome the continual crises of his world. His life consists of creating fiction, and his consciousness is determined by the fiction he creates. He stays alive, he says, "to discover what takes place next in this book" (145). Not only does he create himself by art, he also determines to some degree the nature of the reality with which he must live. Reality in *The Journal of Albion Moonlight* consists of an interaction between what is external and the perceiver. It is not solipsistic, because what is perceived is largely occasioned by causes outside the narrator-author, and it is not entirely deterministic because the artist can summon the powers of the imagination and change reality by creating new perceptions of it. In other words, Albion is developing illuminated artistic models of truth from moment to moment; his book is exactly his consciousness. Unless he simply abandons the book, the reader is forced to experience what Albion experiences, to perceive with Albion's perception. By making his book into a person Albion attempts to prod the sensitive reader into a true (that is, innocent) perception, and thereby to expose him to the profound wrongness of things.

The emphasis on engaging the reader has other important literary consequences. Personalism holds at its core a fundamental experiential knowledge that cannot be taught. Because of the mystical attitude that recognizes truth only as it is apprehended by particular persons, each reader must, in a sense, re-create that knowledge by the activity of his own imagination. The poem inspired by that knowledge, then, becomes the ground on which the imaginations of poet and reader meet, and the reader becomes the necessary ally of the poet in realizing truth. Before the work of art is morally or aesthetically satisfactory—before it can fully exist—it must be re-created by the experience of individual readers. A model for this conspiracy of inspired imaginations, acting independently, spontaneously, and with only the tacit instruction provided by the common experience of the poem (which is a primary sense of the "this" of the first line below) might be found in the passage which culminates Whitman's long strategic approach to the reader in "Crossing Brooklyn Ferry":

> What is more subtle than this which ties me to the woman or
>   man that looks in my face?
> Which fuses me into you now, and pours my meaning into
>   you?
>
> We understand then do we not?
> What I promis'd without mentioning it, have you not
>   accepted?
> What the study could not teach—what the preaching could not
>   accomplish is accomplish'd, is it not?

The creative act demanded of the audience would ideally be as difficult as the poet's own. It thus demands a high degree of spiritual development, which is commonly attributed to a future that contemporaneous culture is in the process of preparing. Whitman, for instance, insisted in "An Old Man's Rejoinder" that "to have great heroic poetry we need great readers—a heroic appetite and audience." Henry Miller assumed a similarly lofty standard.

He envisioned that art would cease to be a separate category of activity and, in its final phase, become life itself—"but for that to become possible man must become thoroughly religious, not a believer, but a prime mover, a god in fact and deed. He will become that inevitably."[12] More playful, but with a similar concern for the future of both his poem and the progress of his audience, is William Carlos Williams's dedication of the personalistic "January Morning,"[13] in which the final line is the kicker:

> All this—
>
>   was for you, old woman
> I wanted to write a poem
> that you could understand
> for what good is it to me
> if you can't understand it?
>   But you got to try hard—

Such personalistic aspirations to the reorientation or evolution of an audience have inspired a number of often negative literary methods which might seem perverse to one trained in more traditional disciplines. Most fundamentally, perhaps, the concept of meaning as an abstractable, verbalizable component of a poem or fiction is either redefined or dismissed by personalistic writers, who are unwilling to postulate a referent for meaning separable from the total experience of the work of art. Meaning, T. S. Eliot says in *The Use of Poetry and the Use of Criticism*, keeps the reader occupied while the poem works upon him.[14] The danger of that approach is that the meaning will be mistaken for the poem—as in Eliot's own work, which to his distress was often read as an inspired intellectual game in which an approved meaning rewarded the diligent researcher. Like the Zen Buddhists, who deliberately make their teaching meaningless, American mystical writers fear that meaning might be seized upon as a way of evading rather than discovering access to the full experience of the poem. In their most ambitious work, they attempt to keep the life of a poem or fiction beyond paraphrase and deny their audience any too easy thematic statement on which reaction might be wasted. Readers of "Song of Myself," *Spring and All*, *The Journal of Albion Moonlight*, or *Tropic of Capricorn* are expected to be more than witnesses. They should consider themselves extensions of the action.

Patchen's typically uncompromising reliance upon the creativity of the reader sometimes develops an obscurity that is more apparent than real. His weaving of the reader into the texture of the poem and the resulting moral and artistic intensity are illustrated in one of his compassionate poems of psychological terror. "The Lute in the Attic" (*Collected Poems* 378) is a monologue addressed by an unidentified speaker to one William Brewster Hollins (Willy) concerning events of which the reader is ignorant. Because the speaker assumes a knowledge of these events in his or her allusive remarks, the reader, who has the poem only as a sort of overheard fragment, is immediately thrust into the center of its situation. With Willy, he is addressed as "you" and expected to react to the strange things of the past with which he is darkly confronted. He is told "things in confidence."

The story involves some crime Willy committed when young, after which he fled the community. Only the primordial nature of his sin—that it was violent and bloody and probably sexual—is made explicit, and the terror of it is dimly suggested by reference to its circumstances and effects: the seven fat ducks with their mouths full of blood, the insanities of Willy's father and Isalina, who lay naked with Willy a few hours before "it" happened, the suggestion that Sam Hanner's alcoholism was caused by watching "it." There is some hint also that Willy's crime betrayed kinship. He is called back to "stand here/ By the fog-blunted house that is silent now," which, with other details, may suggest that the house was that of his family, whose generations were cut off by his act. Later, he is called to "Lie here at the side of your brother," as if justice demanded it. It is even conceivable that Isalina is his sister. With the allusion to the authority of "the Fathers" and the elemental imagery of water, vegetation, and animal life, the unknown event at the center of the poem takes on something of the quality of the earliest, most brutal mythological murders.

The mystery of "The Lute in the Attic" is intensified by the anonymity of the speaker, of whom we can definitely say only that he or she knows Willy intimately, has observed the consequences of his act and brooded about it for many years. The portentousness

of his or her call to Willy, which, with a frightening calmness, is
the characteristic tone of "The Lute in the Attic," is intensified by
the peculiarly appropriate form the poem takes. The first and last
of its five stanzas are parallel invocations, while the middle three
are descriptive. The first stanza issues the opening call, and then
establishes the fundamental situation in free verse lines of varying
length, which fall into a loose parallelism as the shorter lines pick
up and extend the basic image of the longer:

> The apples are red again in Chandler's Valley
> redder for what happened there
> And the ducks move like flocculent clocks
> round and round, and round

The stanza then continues with another, more formal, invocation
of Willy by his full name and a demand that he return to "the fog-
blunted house" he has made sinister. The final two lines hint that
he will be exposed to the full understanding and consequences of
his crime when he again glimpses "these terrible ducks."

In the second, third, and fourth stanzas, the nature of Willy's act
is suggested by its crippling effect upon witnesses. Here, evoca-
tions of intolerable emotion contrast eerily with the speaker's
deliberate calmness, and suggest some only barely restrained in-
sanity in the narrative voice. Then the final stanza, in which a
resolution is at least made possible, parallels the first in form. It
opens with the same line, proceeds to the same summons, repeats
the formal invocation of "William Brewster Hollins" and, like the
first stanza, gives the words "I call you back!" a line of their own,
in contrast to the longer rhythmical unit of the other lines. The first
stanza is also echoed in the demand that Willy return to the place
he has fled—to lie by his brother "here in the rain and the dark
beside the willows/ Hearing the voices of lovers under the flowery
hedge." Other patterns of repetition are completed by the image of
the "seven lean ducks" which replaces the earlier "fat ducks,"
implying that some grisly retribution awaits Willy, and by the final
two lines which, like those of the first stanza, hint at an inevitable
horror—in death as in revenge: "And show you worse things than
your father sees/ And show you things far worse than your father
sees, Willy." The repetition and balances by which the implied
narrative is ended, coupled with the fact that the calling is done

only in the opening and closing stanzas, lend a kind of chantlike and ritualistic quality to the poem. In fact, with their naked anger and anguish Patchen's verses seem akin to the primitive rituals humanity first erected against the moral chaos of its world.

This powerful sense of ritual and the emotion behind it remain unfocused while the speaker remains anonymous. Because whoever is narrating the poem is close to past events we need a firm identification in order to piece them together. Without an attribution we do not understand the significance of details, or know if the pain and anger of the poem are the active emotions of a victim or the resigned emotions of a witness. Perhaps the narrative voice is nothing more than that of a concerned observer, but its relationship to Willy seems more intimate than that, and Patchen probably intends that we involve ourselves by speculating about the matter. One possibility—and the choice is almost purely intuitional—is that the speaker is Willy's mother. She is the only important member of the family not mentioned in the poem, and an occasional phrase, such as "your father," may seem vaguely maternal. By identifying a mother who has survived a family atrocity and yearns for the return of her son so that her agony and his might be completed, we might be able to extend the implications of the poem's title. Of course the lute is primarily a symbol of the lyric art with which humanity has responded to the challenges of failure, death, and the unknown. But it could also be a physical object which has been put away and forgotten, and which, being turned up, triggers a stream of melancholy associations. If we assume that dramatic situation, the lute in the attic becomes as well a psychological metaphor for memory and conscience.

We might also argue that Willy's brother is the speaker. The call from the grave of a spirit that needs revenge before it can rest could explain the maniacal intensity of the poem, the "so much hate" of the final stanza, and the chilling vision of death in the concluding lines. The speaker *could* be the brother, and the identification would be appropriate, but there is no conclusive way to establish it. With all the evidence in, it might as well be a snoopy neighbor, or God, or Willy himself. It might even be Isalina—a narrative turnabout that would not be at all out of keeping with a schizophrenic vision Patchen often employs.

Patchen's failure to identify his narrative voice would be disastrous in a poem aimed at a statement of what events mean. As it stands on the page, however, "The Lute in the Attic" is a sort of raw material which has a meaning only when a reader engages it. We are not asked to decipher Patchen's words so much as to search out our own obscure voices and confess to ourselves our own unspeakable sin. Everyone is liable to the primordial crime of blood and lust that is the subject of the poem, and Patchen's meaning involves the entire process of self-knowledge and purgation by which that crime is brought to consciousness. Because the meaning exists only in the individual it is not paraphrasable. To approximate it, we must remove ourselves so far from the language of the poem that our words cannot affect it. "Know thyself" might be a "meaning" of "The Lute in the Attic." "Be whole" might be another. The purpose of the poem recalls Albion Moonlight's vision of the artist as healer.

The demand "The Lute in the Attic" makes upon the creative reader may be seen more clearly in the earlier "Panel 19" of *Panels for the Walls of Heaven* (retitled "The Builders" in *Collected Poems*). An unsympathetic reader might accuse me of attempting to transmute failure into virtue in my discussion of "The Lute in the Attic," but "Panel 19" quite obviously demands that the reader bring creativity to it and is inchoate until he does. A series of surrealistic images of light, clouds, and mud opens the piece, which is narrated in the first person and defined almost entirely by the progress of a wall that is being built next to the narrator's home. The building of the wall is described in terms of sensual dissociation. At first, the narrator hears the pounding of nails and the grunting of men and horses, and is able to "smell the giant labor," without being able to see what is causing all the commotion. Later he sees the frenzied activity of both men and animals without hearing them. Although it is raining, proximity to the wall exposes him to great heat and, at one point, a mysterious concussion.

As the narrator describes the wall and its bewildering effects upon his senses, he is clearly living in a reality different than his wife's; she finds him dreaming, or sleepwalking, or rolling around in the mud. There are suggestions that he may be insane: he is convinced that his wife is conspiring to hurt him; he sees his dead brother in the fields and at work on the wall; he is led home by an invisible hand and voice. At the most intense moment of the narrative, he finds that his wife does not recognize his presence in the house and sees her weeping over a strange man in their bed. As the narrative ends, the wall is finished and, almost gratuitously, the narrator repeats in inverted order the images with which the poem had begun. Through all of this the narrative is alogical and apparently inconsistent. It seems like raw automatic writing until the reader brings to it an understanding of what has happened that simply is not part of the poem itself. We must recognize that the narrator dies in the course of his narrative but does not know it. In a sense, the reader must share the narrator's agony, experience death (as Patchen understood it during those grim years), and name it for himself. Unless he does so, the poem is stillborn.

The apparent obscurity of "Panel 19" represents the critical problem raised by personalism. That system of shared and shifting identities can be difficult because it results in literary practices with objectives and standards different from those of the traditionally oriented literature for which we have a critical vocabulary. The greatest weakness of the personalistic poem limits it to the weaknesses of its creator, because it cannot be polished to the same degree as the art object, which assumes its own existence after its maker's work is done. But the literature of personalism is strong in its potential for discovering more truth than its creator himself can know. It is not limited to perfection.

Chapter 4

Antiliterature and the

Attack on Formalism

*men seem to have lost the perception of
the instant dependence of form upon soul*
　　　　　—Emerson, "The Poet"

In a characteristically partisan essay, Kenneth Rexroth argued that Kenneth Patchen was a writer of antiliterature, and that his raging attacks on artifice grew out of the conviction that "the practice of literature today is the practice of acquiescence."[1] Patchen did not himself adopt the term "antiliterature," which has perhaps been overworked in recent years, but it corresponds so nicely to his attitude and methods that it would be foolhardy to attempt to invent another term for it. Antiliterature is revolutionary, a literary method of sabotage which is to some degree based on, and directed against, the taste and values of those who are perceived to be in political, economic, and thus cultural power. It attacks the very premises of a particular literature. Patchen's own conduct of that attack becomes for practical purposes an attack on traditional or conventional literary form, because he often uses the terms "literature" and "form" interchangeably and with polemical rather than philosophical reference. His romantic argument about the incompatibility of truth and form is basically that articulated by Van Wyck Brooks in the ruminations on the journal discussed earlier, but Patchen's mistrust is more radical and angry than Brooks's, and his denunciations more sweeping.

Patchen feels not only that traditional form reflects the compromise made and demanded by writers he regards as enemies, but also that it provides rhetorical models for timid or compulsive sensibilities. The construction of balanced verbal patterns, he would argue, is mechanical, trivial, and sterile. Such attitudes are familiar enough from the great lovers' quarrel between classicism and romanticism that has informed Western culture for the past two centuries. However, Patchen's unusual vehemence was provoked more immediately by the peculiar historical circumstances of World War II, when an openly aristocratic and reactionary formalism became an important intellectual force in the United States. Writers disappointed by the defeat of the various ideological alliances and communal enterprises of the Great Depression, and alarmed by the exploitation of artistic idealism by totalitarian systems, turned in substantial numbers to the study of tradition and the cultivation of technique. An aestheticism that had lain all but dormant since the late twenties reasserted itself in arguments that literature was essentially amoral and disinterested, and that artists should let social and moral causes alone. Such writers and their allied critics cherished a dispassionate purity of form above all else, or so a hostile observer might perceive them, and Patchen consequently fixed on form and formalism as primary targets.

His quarrel with form is most clearly expressed in the literary discussions scattered throughout *The Journal of Albion Moonlight*. Here form is a traditional or even anachronistic limitation imposed upon the artist, by which content is stifled. As a projection of the dispassionately analytical mind, it is of a piece with the insane desire for logic, the need for even a false sense of continuity, and the rage for order that arises from fear of both experience and freedom. Form is for the comfortable or squeamish; it is artificial in the pejorative sense—as is literature itself. "Literature is what you write when you think you should be saying something," Albion says in distinguishing it from writing; "writing begins when you'd rather be doing something else: and you've just done it" (18). The masters of literature are valuable because they are also great writers: "We must keep Shakespeare and Dostoievsky, because they talked above the clamor of their characters— they poked their bleeding heads through the junk-pile of literature, *and we saw their white, twitching faces*" (201).

Because traditional form is based upon philosophies that have lent themselves to the authoritarian perpetuation of the status quo, as Patchen would continue, it also inhibits or obscures the resolution of moral issues. Especially as it leads to catharsis, it weakens the emotional impact of human misery, thereby providing aesthetic solutions to moral problems and violating the spontaneity of natural perception. It is thus a compromise with historical failure and evil itself. Perhaps an example of the pernicious uses of literary form might result from speculating about the possible treatment of any of a number of recent political assassinations, whether of Gandhi, Kennedy, King, or Sadat. Once, the violence done to great spiritual or national leaders would have been matter for tragedy, and to cast these bloody affairs as tragedies would discover a certain propriety (however unpleasant) in them. If the play were skillfully done, the observer would be purged of his horror at the event and left calm. It would have this comforting effect because the tragic form is based on a fatalistic concept that explains the logic of suffering and violence. Patchen would say—and doubtless most would agree—that such a literary interpretation would muffle the significance of the murder and deprive us of the outraged sense of the absurd by which we understand much of the failure of our time. For Patchen, however—and perhaps here his attitudes become difficult—an elegy would be equally inappropriate. He contends that a deadly blunting of moral and emotional honesty is built into any derivative form, because its relevance is dependent chiefly on the need of insecure people to fit experience to familiar patterns, appropriate or not, in order to understand it. "The world is in a mess," Albion Moonlight explains, "precisely because a bunch of stuffy fools insist there be no mess" (120).

Finally, Patchen believes that artistic form can damage the act of perception itself. Because we have learned how and what to see from previous generations, our perception is conditioned by mistakes made in the prehistory of the race and given permanent authority partly by art. Albion asserts that "the man animal got started on the wrong foot" when he chose badly among the "millions of possible *seeings*" and fixed his error in his head and his culture as truth (298). It is according to this inappropriate choice, reflected in the paintings on the walls of the ancestral caves and incorporated into all the subsequent pictures by which we know the past, that we model our perception of the present.

The idea behind Patchen's distaste for traditional form is at least as old in the United States as Ralph Waldo Emerson's "The American Scholar." For Emerson the only real issue is freedom. His insistence that the American artist abandon old forms for the fresh perceptions made possible by life in a new world is, of course, echoed in the ideas of Walt Whitman, with his fulminations against both political and artistic "feudalism" and his contempt for the merely literary. "No one," Whitman wrote in "A Backward Glance O'er Travel'd Roads," "will get at my verses who insists upon viewing them as literary performance, or attempt at such performance, or as aiming mainly toward art or aestheticism." It is not necessary to linger over passages from Emerson and Whitman, whose struggles to be rid of the restrictions of traditional European culture are well documented. But the legacy of their impulse to antiliterature, a term that undoubtedly would have shocked both men, is illustrated by the lines Allen Ginsberg chose from "Song of Myself" as a motto for *Howl*: "Unscrew the locks from the doors!/ Unscrew the doors themselves from their jambs!"

Among twentieth-century mystical writers, the theory and practice of antiliterature became more self-conscious and sophisticated, partly in response to non-American intellectual movements. After World War I antiliterature had a name and a body of precedent. It could both reconcile and encourage a writer to the paradox of creative work in a deteriorating world. Henry Miller assumed an exemplary modern antiliterary stance in his "Reflections on Writing": "I have always welcomed the dissolving influences [in art]. In an age marked by dissolution, liquidation seems to me a virtue, nay a moral imperative. Not only have I never felt the least desire to conserve, bolster up or buttress anything, but I might say that I have always looked upon decay as being just as wonderful and rich an expression of life as growth."[2] Miller's cheerfulness is more unrelieved than most, but is still characteristic of the surprisingly good-natured sense of health and purpose American mystical writers discover in the antiliterary posture. Wallace Stevens's famous comment on William Carlos Williams is another example: "His passion for the anti-poetic is a blood-passion and not a passion of the inkpot. The anti-poetic is his spirit's cure. He needs it as a naked man needs shelter or as an animal needs salt. To a man with a sentimental side the anti-poetic is that truth, that reality to which all of us are forever fleeing."[3]

In *I Wanted to Write a Poem*, her bibliographical study in collaboration with Williams, Edith Heal described how even after many years the poet still resented Stevens's remarks.[4] While honoring Williams's distaste for being called "anti" anything, we can still acknowledge the shrewdness of Stevens's assessment. Because he wrestled all his life with the misappellations and poetic traditions of the European literary culture to which T. S. Eliot and Ezra Pound turned, Williams stands in opposition to a whole way of literature. In such early experiments as *Kora in Hell*, *Spring and All*, and *The Great American Novel*, he used linguistic and literary conventions in order to subvert them and so to clear the ground for a new kind of writing. In *Paterson* and other later works he explored the simultaneity of destruction and creation in his great theme of descent. Further, he explained much of the revolutionary impulse of antiliterature when he said of *The Tempers*: "The orderliness of verse appealed to me—as it must to any man—but even more I wanted a new order. I was positively repelled by the old order which, to me, amounted to restriction."[5]

Like Williams, Patchen owed much of the method by which he conducted his antiliterary campaigns to the European artistic movements of the period between the wars, and their revolutionary "isms" perhaps encouraged the emergence of the Whitmanian traditionalist. David Gascoyne, introducing Patchen to an English audience in 1946, attempted to explain his characteristic violence, strangeness, and nonsense by naming him "the lone one-man DADA of contemporary America."[6] Gascoyne's analogy to the anarchistic antimovement that attacked art (or, perhaps more accurately, artistry) as simply another bourgeois institution, and discovered integrity in the violently absurdist gesture, can also be applied to the intellectual enthusiasms of the young Williams, whose *Autobiography* is bright in its early years with the names of Man Ray and Marcel Duchamp. Neither Patchen nor Williams, however, could conceivably follow dada to its logical conclusion, as Duchamp did when he abandoned creativity altogether. Patchen's work, in fact, parallels the actual history of dada, which was eventually subsumed by surrealism. His affinity with that movement should be clarified by Georges Le Maître's description of the surrealist program:

> According to the Surrealists, the liberation of our subconscious mind can best be effected through an attitude of deliberate censorship towards all the accepted forms of traditional thinking. . . . Therefore, all means are legitimate which might bring about its [intellect's] total and final disintegration. Irony, ridicule, sarcasm are our most efficient weapons in this struggle for our complete inward enfranchisement. Every fixed form of opinion or expression must be discarded as arbitrary and absurd. Every established law about aesthetics or morals must be ruthlessly swept away. . . . Surrealist humor is a grotesque parody of all things in which the ordinary "unenlightened" man still implicitly believes. . . . When destructive humor has definitely cleared the field of all conventional obstacles, man can at last have access to the enthralling *Surreal*. . . . Of course such contact cannot take place if we look at the world analytically. . . . We must grasp through mystic intuition the totality of energies offered to our experience. . . . Thus would be resolved the age-long antagonism between the subjective and objective.[7]

This is not to say that Patchen was in any sense an orthodox or committed surrealist. His use of European systems was typically eclectic, and he occasionally displayed some impatience with surrealism and its propaganda—at which Albion Moonlight takes his usual tough-minded swipe: "There is no such thing as superrealism. (The surrealists have managed to put on a pretty good show for the middle-class; *but there isn't a religious man among them*)" (307).[8]

Patchen uses his antiliterary tools, both thematic and stylistic, much as a boxer uses his jab: to test the reader's defenses, to weaken them, to keep the attention occupied while he winds up a literary haymaker. One of his most explicit and extensive treatments of the theme of antiliterature is found in *Memoirs of a Shy Pornographer*, with its use of literary society as a setting and its description of the effect of publication of his commercially mutilated book upon the author-hero. Albert Budd, the title character, writes an innocent romance which unscrupulous publishers turn vile by replacing key nouns and verbs with asterisks. As a new literary lion (one of the important settings of *Memoirs* is the archetypal cocktail party), Budd is forced to act out the role of pornographic hero by the assorted harpies and nymphomaniacs who inhabit the fringes of the literary scene, and *Memoirs* becomes, like its great prototype *Don Quixote*, an investigation into the relationship between literary and social role. Like Cervantes's antihero, Albert Budd is given an identity by literature, and its consequence is death. *Memoirs* thus attempts to turn an entire literature in upon itself in order to demonstrate the perniciousness of it and the cultural milieu it reflects.

The antiliterary theme is so prominent throughout Patchen's career that to linger over it might belabor the obvious. His ideological jabbing can be examined and described more immediately as it informs his technique. One of the important devices by which the reader is kept off balance from moment to moment toys with his expectations of what literature is and the continuity he should anticipate from it. In his review of *Selected Poems*, the sympathetic Frajam Taylor took occasion to deplore the perverse puckishness of a mind that could produce "For Whose Adornment":[9]

> For whose adornment the mouths
> Of roses open in languorous speech;
> And from whose grace the trees of heaven
> Learn their white standing.
>
> (I must go now to cash in the milk bottles
> So I can phone somebody
> For enough money for our supper.)

But such deflating anticlimax is both characteristic and pervasive.

Patchen also exploits his reader's sense of continuity and propriety in evoking the preternatural terror that haunts much of his writing. *The Journal of Albion Moonlight*, for instance, opens with a suspiciously sentimental juxtaposition of the natural and supernatural worlds: "The angel lay in a little thicket. It had no need of love; there was nothing anywhere in the world could startle it—we can lie here with the angel if we like." To this point Patchen offers his reader a kind of greeting-card sentiment. The thought is obviously about to be completed by some spiritual truism. But the next phrase—"It couldn't have hurt much when they slit its throat"—jars the reader out of any complacency he might have been so ill advised as to permit himself. The technique of enticing the reader to the edge of a literary precipice and then booting him over not only disabuses him; it also traps him within the surface of the fiction. Because he is lost in a world of shattered forms where the future is unpredictable and even the past subject to change, he is forced to cling to Patchen as guide.

Parody can be used to induce similar processes of disorientation and redefinition. Thematically, parody mocks approved literary styles, and although few contemporary writers of note escape Patchen's jabs, his favorite targets are James Joyce and Ernest Hemingway, probably the most influential prose stylists of our era. At the same time the parodist is whacking at established reputations, aping the old ways of expression, and jeering at old orthodoxies, he undermines, once again, the conventional responses to literature. When he is successful, he leaves the reader a victim of his own sophistication. Early in the *Journal* Albion Moonlight embarks on a long mockery of literary criticism by interpreting his own characters allegorically. Because we are still in the first stages of the narrative, in need of a key to its complexities, the parody is not readily apparent, and we follow Albion's exegesis with some interest until he explodes into a denunciation of categorization and the search for meaning—"All this rot about who is what! Why must you look for bed-time story significances in everything? . . . Take what I give you . . . Billy Delian is no more Hitler than you are . . . When Hitler comes into this record he will come as Hitler. I want that understood: things are what I say they are" (31).

Patchen also parodies authorial attempts to develop meaning. In *Memoirs* he incorporates one of his criticisms of surrealism into a parody of classic Freudian symbolism, in which burlesque detail makes the portentousness of surrealistic or psychoanalytic literature seem obvious. The Diver (whose name is suggestive, but who is never assigned a precise parodic value) tells Budd about "a building on Madison in the fifties where 400 elevator boys live in a large room in the basement unknown to the superintendent, despite the fact that two old darkies go down there every night and teach them tap-dancing" (12). This persistent definition by parody is meant to do more than amuse or mock; it should also force the reader to test his own reactions. If he reads Patchen well, he will at some point ask himself if he is attending properly to the page before him or whether he has slipped into making stock responses.

For all the satisfaction Patchen obviously takes in such tactics, they are finally only tactical. At least in the middle period, when antiliterature is a major concern, his strategy is better reflected in his massive attacks on the overall form of a fiction, as if he were attempting to breach the last defenses his culture had erected against insight and innocence. This assault culminates in *Sleepers Awake*. It may be impossible that anything except an antiliterary approach can provide access to this big, smoky literary bastard, which is so successful in denying the reader his expectations that it can be understood only in terms of artistic deterioration and the failure of logic. Even the violent antistructure, the confused discontinuity, of *Sleepers Awake*, however, is appropriate to its concern with the difficulties and dangers that frustrate the writer. The moral and physical assassination of the poet is one of the most important of the grim thematic strands that are woven into the deranged surface of Patchen's book. To the extent that it coordinates an impulse, *Sleepers Awake* is about—and is—a work of art struggling to come into being. It is the record of the attempt at its own creation as an imitation of truth. The enterprise fails, finally, because of the stubborn, efficient malice of a world and a time.

The narrator of *Sleepers Awake* (the author and hero also) is Almar Gnunsn. I suspect that the name puns on *alma*, new son, and noon sun, thus invoking the arisen god, but the word play seems more than a little tone-deaf. As a visionary, pilgrim, representative human being, and artist, Almar has much in common with the Albion Moonlight of the early *Journal*. In the opening narrative sequence (7–66), which ends as the first internal novel begins, his great motivation and at least a substantial part of his identity are expressed in his pilgrimage toward "The Mystery." Like Albion, he is the mystical soul trapped in a world of war; his journey in search of secret knowledge and ecstatic consciousness is described in heavily biblical language. He is also a great lover who attempts to perpetuate and share his visionary idealities by bringing them into flesh. His lovemaking with the woman accompanying him is not only an emotional fulfillment; it is also a high creativity, and the first narrative moves toward the birth to the lovers of a miraculous Christlike child. But like Albion also, Almar is a man involved in human failure, and he has the telltale habit of accepting the dominant identity of those around him. During his travels over a mythological war landscape, he encounters repeatedly the primordial enactments of deceit and brutality, and sometimes responds by assuming a depraved personality. Again like Albion, he characteristically sins as a rapist and murderer.

The world Almar confronts shifts abruptly between symbolic landscapes of war and those of religious peace, both of which take many specific settings. As he writes, Almar mimetically shifts his subject with them, but without warning or explanation. The only rule he seems to respect with regard to narrative is that it shall not be completed. Stories and anecdotes begun in this first section are dropped, either to remain unfinished or to be continued later, if the reader is astute enough to recognize them when they reappear in their altered forms. Almar's identity, of course, keeps pace with the various realities and tones of his narrative. He is incarnated in a number of selves, which correspond to the possible range of reaction to his world. However, in this section as throughout the book, Almar's most important roles are of the holy man and the wisecracking tough guy, who appears in numerous parodies of the hard-boiled school of detective fiction. This latter figure is a favorite of Patchen's, and he is more closely related to the religious character than is obvious at first glance. The detective is a seeker after truth, a conqueror of illusion, and a lone worker of justice. His representatives in *Sleepers Awake* resemble the brave figure of which Albert Budd dreams near the end of *Memoirs of a Shy Pornographer*: the "Public Detective" who will work "To search out the ways of the Mystery—To hunt down all the clues which may lead men to that level where the Answer is—where God is—and where everything is done in purity and innocence to the end that all men may live in peace and love the Beautiful together" (241). Whether Almar is playing the detective or the saint, however, he is always the creator. The birth of his child is a renewal of the holiness and redemptiveness of Christ, and represents one of Almar's attempts to create out of love a truth which the world will have despite itself. When people ignore the birth and thus lose its potential power (suggesting Patchen's idea that the creative act is not sufficient unto itself), Almar turns to another kind of creativity and begins the novel of "The Man with the Detachable Brainpan."

Almar's novel fictionalizes some of his most pressing emotional needs and is important especially at the beginning and end of *Sleepers Awake*, but it is fragmentary and occasionally lost for long stretches.[10] The hero is Aloysius Best, man of letters and inventor, who has developed a pacifist machine of unexplained magical properties and attempts a literary transmutation that will make reality holy. At the behest of Louie, an angel who speaks for the authorial conscience and frequently interrupts the narrative to urge him on, Aloysius writes the fiction in which he appears in order to organize a voyage away from war to a calm region where his invention can be put to use. His passenger list is made up of literary types, who are aware that Best is their creator; but the antiliterary fever finally infects even them. They escape his control and behave badly. With his characters in a sort of mutiny, Best's yacht runs into a wildly typographical storm (see pp. 84–85) and sinks.

Despite the symbolism of shipwreck, Aloysius and his characters do not drown. Because of the weight of the paraphernalia Aloysius has aboard they sink rapidly into an underwater bubble which houses several strange new worlds. The inhabitants are not human, but their worlds, as might be expected, are simply slightly distorted versions of the world which Almar fights in his own narratives. Aloysius and his friends are alternately tormented and pampered, initiated into new ways of love and served food of the most unappetizing sorts. The inquisitors of the submarine world torture Aloysius until he is psychologically broken and hears his own voice screaming in the distance. At the same time, both his captors and his former shipmates offer him revelations that take him closer to the mystery of life and death. As he attempts to bring these new perspectives together, he is tried by his old acquaintances as a criminal artist. He is executed by a clumsy policeman, and he leaves the book with an injunction to "go into the darkness as clean as you can for Christ's sake" (380).

Besides the more or less autobiographical efforts of Aloysius and Almar, *Sleepers Awake* contains numerous other fictional attempts to confront the contemporary world. Aloysius Best's novel-within-a-novel, for instance, tells the alternately parodic and pathetic story of the love between Thane Chillingsdale and Tranquil Flume (both characters from other parts of the book) as another example of the attempts of human beings to bend reality by force of will. Thane is accidentally killed by a hunter before Tranquil's eyes, and the story deals with Tranquil's refusal either to be comforted or to admit that he is dead. She believes that she can keep him alive by the simple power of faith, and to some degree she succeeds. At the end of her narrative she encounters Thane in the night, whether as hallucination or in some reality we are not told. But the antiliterary character of the book interrupts her as it does the others; just as Thane is about to explain something of the mystery, the narrative breaks off, never to be resumed.

These failures of art and creativity in *Sleepers Awake* are all directly or indirectly attributable to war, because in wartime no logic or sequence is possible. Patchen refuses to allow the presence of a beginning, middle, and end in anything but an occasional vignette. Even the identity and values of the writer change without warning or explanation. In the collapse of structure and design the surface of the narrative often becomes nearly unreadable. It is made up of fragments of speech, scraps of parody, unidentified interjections, and framed slogans set in various types. The only agency of communication finally left is the raised voice, and the narrators of *Sleepers Awake* break again and again into shrill, raging, typographically extravagant statements of their wrath or sorrow. These agonized outbursts embody the final desperate determination that the human voice be heard above the roar of the war machines.

Both the loudest and angriest of the protesting voices is Almar Gnunsn's, and *Sleepers Awake* is unmistakably his book. Other narrative efforts start off briskly and develop their own direction, but they drop away abruptly to a vision of Almar and the cycle of experience in which he finds himself. It is as if he were personally beneath all the literary smoke screens which drift through the book, as if we caught through gaps in the cover glimpses of his situation as the reality on which *Sleepers Awake* is grounded. As we read on, alternately baffled and annoyed by Almar's alogical reappearances, we gradually gather by a kind of osmosis some idea of what his reality is. In either of his primary identities—pilgrim saint or tough detective—he is trapped in a nightmarish series of events which recur inexorably, but in slightly altered form and with greater or lesser elaboration of detail. In fact, we may say that they are dreams, that reality is dream, and Almar's attempt to waken from the feverish dreaming of the race is one reference for the book's title. His dilemma is similar to that posed in Whitman's "The Sleepers" or Williams's *Paterson*, but its outcome is not so happy as theirs.

One of Almar's recurrent scenes takes place in a diner where he complains imaginatively about the coffee and quarrels with the counterman, who has the quirk of being unable to pronounce the name of a popular cigarette except as "Chesterfeds." In this scene Almar is a tough-talking fugitive who has a price on his head and is in danger of betrayal by the counterman (or, occasionally, the waitress). Like all the basic scenes, this one goes nowhere and eventually develops a nearly unbearable tension.

Another of the basic scenes of *Sleepers Awake* illustrates a characteristic Jungian imagery. It finds Almar walking in a vast expanse of space—over broad fields or through mountains. As the fugitive, he is alone; as the holy man, he is usually accompanied by his spiritual wife. Both figures, however, are lonely, and for both the scene is maddening. Landscapes that are peaceful on their surface are also alive with hidden presences, who subject Almar to unspeakable psychological ordeals and destroy whatever beauty or security he is after. The action is reported in a slow, portentous prose which gives the narrative a grimly dreamlike texture—in Almar's description, for instance, of the "flowers" and "bubbles" breaking out on the faces of the six young men who do not react to their unexplained murder (280–81). The expansively spatial setting also suggests that Almar is unable to find any hiding place.

The flight scenes, with their sweatiness, cruelty, and shadowy motivation, are complemented by another group of primary scenes in which Almar plays the sinister sexual partner. His rapes and murders, which are only flashed on the consciousness, associate him with a collective guilt, and he characteristically performs them against his will, then runs. Almar's sexual role is not preponderantly negative, however; more often he expresses a capacity for absolute love, and another of the recurrent scenes takes place in bed. At these times Almar is either the spiritual lover or the cynically defensive, but essentially innocent and hopeful, man of the world. But neither spirituality nor cynicism is adequate. Like the others, these scenes break off abruptly in blood or frustration. The loss of the love partner, either because of the shiftings of dream reality or because of a suddenly fatal violence, is Almar's most intense suffering.

One other repeatedly significant scene is the meeting with Old Zenaslufski, who is commonly known, perhaps symbolically, as old Zen, and whose appearances coordinate all of Almar's basic characterizations, settings, and thematic concerns. In his most important encounter with Old Zen (295–320), Almar acts out his entire sequence of roles. As the panicky fugitive, he escapes from a plain, and reaches Zen's cabin in the mountains, where the old man is dying. Almar alternately nurses and torments his host, and in turn is sometimes horribly attacked and sometimes treated to interludes of rare innocent beauty by Zen's frequent visitors. Zenaslufski himself seems to be related to the wise old man of Jungian archetypology, but his wisdom does not coincide with Almar's needs, and he occasionally takes on a vaguely sinister quality. Although his narrative has details that could be worked into alternate interpretations, he may embody something of the failed wisdom of the past, especially as Almar ends his story by burying him.

These fundamental scenes, frenzied but unchanging, comprise one reality to which much of the seriousness of *Sleepers Awake* can be related. Not only do they function as a sort of framed image in their own right, but also they—or, more properly, their components—inform other sections of the text as well. Characters' names, fragments of physical description, identifiable turns of speech, and allusions to events already described crop up everywhere, creating a suspension of time, a system of reference and cross-reference in which all events are one event and all language flows from a central dream reality. The antiliterary rerun of scenes, with its sabotage of attempts at larger form, exposes Almar's character starkly and justifies his obsessive wrestling with his situation.

Much of the significance of that situation is summed up in the book's concluding sequence (382–89). Here Almar is again the fugitive, returning again to the diner. The law has offered a large reward for his capture, and he knows fatalistically that he is quickly to be sold, apprehended, and executed. As time runs out, he involves himself in a poignantly comic interlude with a lady and a butler by trying to help a hurt puppy. His attempt is unsuccessful, and when the dog runs off he is simply left waiting, without even the cheap favors of the diner's waitress for comfort. The story, as always, breaks off at this point, but the implications are unavoidable. Almar's last words are: "I opened my mouth to maybe say a bit of a prayer for them [probably his assassins-to-be]. And it started to bleed again."

Patchen's manipulations are ingenious, and Almar Gnunsn becomes a genuinely interesting character as we accumulate glimpses of him beneath the wispy smoke of his narrative, but *Sleepers Awake* finally doesn't come off. It lacks unity, which is a virtue even in antiliterature, and it fails to provide the reader any firm orientation, even negative, by which he can pick his way through its intricacies. Although several of its extended anecdotes are among the most successful achievements of both Patchen's vulgarity and his peculiar style of parody (the story, for instance, of C. F. Lemson and the boy with the lollypop, pp. 93–95), its humor is not sustained in narrative and remains local and rather too flippant. In a sense, *Sleepers Awake* accomplishes its purpose too well; its antiliterary method is so purely applied that the book is for practical purposes readable only by aficionados after extended preparation.

In general, antiliterature succeeds as a negative way of exposing the reader to a positive experience, such as the transcendent presence of the poet, Albion Moonlight. But in *Sleepers Awake* there is no truly positive source of strength. The book is all jab and no punch. Almar Gnunsn has neither the integrity nor the dignity of the Whitmanian artist. He is more the passive victim than Albion is. Lacking any great solidity or genuine possibility of human victory at their heroic center, the precariously sustained narrative relationships of *Sleepers Awake* simply collapse. The book thus becomes an anthology and a testimony, rather than the masterpiece that one feels is struggling to emerge on almost every page.

Chapter 5

After Antiliterature:

Organicism and the

Rediscovery of Form

Yes, the imagination, drunk with prohibitions, has destroyed and recreated everything afresh in the likeness of that which it was. Now indeed men look about in amazement at each other with a full realization of the meaning of "art."

—Williams, *Spring and All*

Even in the crazy, violent first pages of his early manifesto, William Carlos Williams kept his reader aware that the negative and destructive aspects of literary activity, no matter how morally purposeful, would not in themselves suffice. In fact, the poems of *Spring and All*, which arose, as it were, to the challenge of its apocalyptic prose, were immediately turned to images of natural renewal and the figure of "the farmer—composing/ —antagonist." We might reap the implications of Williams's metaphors by suggesting that the use of the antiliterary mode is like plowing the old harvest under and fertilizing the harrowed earth. It is in a sense only the necessary first cycle in the process of organicism, and it should be partly judged according to its flowerings in the subsequent regenerative cycle. That orientation to an organic rhythm and logic, with its insistence that the form of any writing must grow as spontaneously and unself-consciously according to intrinsic law as a natural life or thing, is one of the fundamental postures that Emerson and Whitman bequeathed to future generations.

Williams's own *Paterson* is an exemplary organic poem. Williams "let form take care of itself," as he observed, by following the course of a river to the sea and pacing the verse according to the pace of local speech.[1] John Steinbeck described the composition of the narrative of *Sea of Cortez* in similar terms: "We have a book to write about the Gulf of California. We could do one of several things about its design. But we have decided to let it form itself: its boundaries a boat and a sea; its duration a six weeks' charter time; its subject everything we could see and think and even imagine; its limits—our own without reservation."[2] In "Reflections on Writing" Henry Miller interpreted his work according to a series of natural metaphors which are reminiscent of Whitman's. "I drop my fruits like a ripe tree," he wrote; "I would like my words to flow along in the same way that the world flows along, a serpentine movement through incalculable dimensions, axes, latitudes, climates, conditions." He continued later: "Like the spider, I return again and again to the task, conscious that the web I am spinning is made of my own substance, that it will never fail me, never run dry."[3] Such examples from both mystical and more generally romantic sources could easily be multiplied, but it may be more useful here to consider an example of what organic form is not. Its priorities may be negatively illustrated by reference to Thomas Wolfe, the shape of whose autobiographical novels, especially the unedited *Of Time and the River*, might be considered derivative, because they follow the chronology of their author's life rather mechanically and automatically, and reveal no attempt to discover the peculiar law by which as stories they must be told.

Kenneth Patchen's organicism is often more radical, and consequently more troublesome, than that of his contemporaries. At least in his long fictions, he permits his work its head so stubbornly that it is not subject to any external formal or generic limitation; it is not even always limited to writing. The major prose fictions, for instance, are not novels. *The Journal of Albion Moonlight*, *Sleepers Awake*, and *Memoirs of a Shy Pornographer* are mixed forms of the romance, among the scarce modern examples of successful prose narrative with a significant admixture of verse. In all three books, Patchen moves easily from prose into a long Whitmanian verse line, usually reserved for moments of prophecy or intense emotion. He also uses much prose-poetry, so that his mixed forms are rarely one thing or the other, and he is able to shift immediately into either poetry or prose without disrupting the flow of his narrative. The graceful movement between genres at critical moments is especially effective in *Memoirs of a Shy Pornographer.*

Patchen also expresses his organicism by combining his linguistic element with a pictorial element which becomes integral to the structures of *The Journal of Albion Moonlight*, *Sleepers Awake*, and many poems. In *The Journal* a long Whitmanian oration about the blight war has brought to earth builds to an outburst of wildly denunciatory prophecies of revenge and death. The alternately lustful and fearful anticipation of dreadful justice is expressed in images of execution which, at the climax of the poem, become a visual-verbal symbol for much of the terror of the entire *Journal*. Patchen blocks his words into the rough shape of a gallows, then adds a drawing for which:[4]

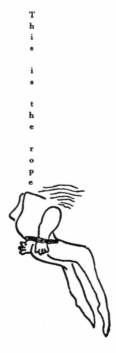

Sleepers Awake relies more heavily on its visual component. The storm which sinks Aloysius Best and his mutinous shipmates, for instance, gradually takes over Aloysius's writing until the typography resembles the crashing rise and fall of the waves, and the descriptions of activities aboard ship are suddenly compressed into a symbolic picture of the entire situation (see fig. 1). Such attempts to mate linguistic and visual elements in these works of the forties are often daring, always interesting, but rarely wholly successful. As always, reading Patchen is a little like playing an aesthetic slot machine.

The organic principle also functions in the so-called mystical structure, the abstracted and idealized pattern of development into which the records of mystical lives regularly fall. Although other numerical divisions are occasionally encountered, the five-fold progression of mystical consciousness is the most common and widely accepted. It was first identified by Evelyn Underhill,[5] but for our purposes it is probably better to repeat the description Patchen himself gives in an introduction to a 1947 edition of William Blake's *Job*. Patchen's categories resemble Underhill's, but he has different names for them: "There are five stages of the Mystic Road (*and no mystic but has experienced them*): 1) Gaining a sense of the Divine; 2) The emptying of Self; 3) Return to the Divine; 4) 'The Dark Night of the Soul'—torture of Self in separation from God; 5) The Total Identification with the All-Highest [or] 1) Birth (taste); 2) Hardship (smell); 3) Maturity (sight); 4) Decadence (hearing); 5) Transformation (touch)."[6]

Patchen's schematization of mystical biography—the very fact that it can be schematized—might seem to indicate that it is itself simply another conventionalized survival of life that can be applied to literary works as a prefabricated form. However, neither mysticism nor organicism preclude the activity of the intellect, with its awareness of pattern and category, and its invaluable capacity for introspection. In fact, we may argue that a truly organic aesthetic is obliged in some way to provide for the abstractive, ordering genius of the intellect if it is to respect the intrinsic law of human generation. Further, the five-fold structure is an approximated pattern of observed behavior and not in itself a discipline. Mystics do not aspire to follow the pattern. Rather it grows inevitably out of their life and work, reconstructing the

150

Figure 1: *Sleepers Awake* (150–51)

—"T   o   d r e
a
    m   you   s   e e   a g
r e a t   l i   g h   t,   i
  s   a
    h
a p
                        p
                    y   p   re   sage;
it denotes
            th   a   t   yo
    u   w
            ill   att

151

natural configurations of mystical experience. By the same organic law, an authentic mystical structure is not dispassionately fabricated by an author, but is the informing quality in his work, identified and interpreted according to the similarity it intrinsically bears to the examples of other mystics. It is important to recognize the difference. Failure to distinguish between a set form and the untidy, inconsistent pattern of development that can be dug out and reconstructed from a record of individual experience is responsible for much confusion about mystical writing. The contradictions in a recent critical debate about the form of "Song of Myself" provide one example, so that a reading of this heterogeneous masterpiece, which has resisted critical classification, should help us approach Patchen's own variations on mystical structure. "Song of Myself" is particularly valuable in demonstrating how the five-fold mystical form works, rather than how it means. The distinction is essential to Patchen as well as Whitman. Their form is dynamic, a function of motion rather than a system of fixed reference.

Two influential recent studies of Whitman's great poem are by Malcolm Cowley and James E. Miller, Jr., both of whom read it as a mystical record, but with radical disagreement about the logic of an implicit narrative sequence. Miller's traditionally oriented reading examines "Song of Myself" as an inverted mystical experience, in which Whitman describes seven stages of unfolding mystical consciousness. This analysis follows Underhill's model, except that Miller allows additional sections for entrance to and departure from the mystical state, and he argues that the stages of illumination (Patchen's "Return to the Divine") and the dark night of the soul occur simultaneously in sections 33–37. Cowley is more descriptive and less traditional. He divides the poem into eight related groups which grow naturally from the ecstasy described in section 5. Like Miller, he disclaims any intention of imposing patterns and is aware of the problem of confusing artificial and organic form. However, he argues for a logic of narrative order that would be violated by any other sequence. Both critics, then, assert that Whitman had a distinct structural foundation upon which he built his poem and according to which it can be analyzed.[7]

Despite their basic agreement, Miller and Cowley might almost be discussing different poems. Perhaps we are not forced to choose between them. V. K. Chari, an Indian scholar studying Whitman from the viewpoint of Vedanta, takes issue with both critics for what he considers their imposition of arbitrary divisions upon the poem, and he rejects their insistence that it develops themes logically toward a climax. Chari argues that the poem cannot be categorized or analyzed, that it is formless because it can be related to no structural principle outside of its own existence. He sees it as essentially a series of variations on the theme of identity without any particular order of succession, and although his judgment is extreme, it represents one of the most common critical attitudes toward "Song of Myself."[8]

The compromise by which I would ease these disagreements is less ingenious and courageous than the structural analyses of Cowley and Miller, and it lacks the austerity of Chari's Vedantic epistemology. I would discover the traditional five mystical stages in "Song of Myself," but not as the principle by which Whitman consciously organized it. The process of mystical development is not the form, but a metaphor by which we suggest the form. By schematizing mystical experience we create points of reference for loose groupings of more or less related material. As students of mysticism and literature, we can then name the groupings with some profit to ourselves, but little relevance to Whitman's immediate purpose, which was surely rather expressionistic than interpretive or dramatic.

The first major division of "Song of Myself" includes sections 1–5[9] and can be compared to Patchen's initial "Gaining a sense of the Divine." In this sequence Whitman celebrates his own sensual and transcendental capacities, makes promises to his reader, and hints at intimacies with God and God's secrets. Despite his confident expansiveness, however, he also begins his poem in a condition of alienation from the day-to-day routine of society, and he is forced to distinguish between the mock "Me" who is involved in the social "pulling and hauling" and the true "Me myself" who is the detached, universalized observer of such activities. This dualism of self is objectified in the schizophrenic vision of the fourth section, which introduces a critical imagery for American mystical writing[10] and poses the problem of identity the poem must solve. In immediate reaction to that description of alienation and personal dissociation, the famous visionary rapture of section 5 provides the poem's first instance of union, with its overtones of erotic fulfillment, universal identity, and omniscience. Although this section culminates the initial interplay between soul and body, and establishes the pervasiveness of cosmic love, Whitman clearly did not intend that it settle the truths or resolve the tensions of the poem. It is too easily—indeed, involuntarily—attained, and it is significantly transient. Rather than achievement of the unitive state, it represents a conversion, in which the beauty and power of the mystery are for the first time glimpsed. Because the mystic is not yet ready to sustain supernal rapture, he must abandon it, and it remains a goal which he strives to recapture and make permanent.

The second mystical stage, corresponding to sections 6–23 of "Song of Myself," is the "emptying of Self." Although the process is not particularly tortuous, in this sequence Whitman purges himself of "the other I am" who is involved in the social games of "pulling and hauling." The two sections about death that open this phase of the poem are appropriate psychological and physiological reactions to the detumescence that follows the erotic union of section 5. Following them, the sequence is composed largely of catalogs. The poet sheds his mundane self by identifying with the larger life of which he is part: with a range of typical American personalities in one series (section 10), and with an assortment of natural creatures in another (section 14). By suppressing his ego and abandoning individual attributes, he builds to an ultimately democratic denial of the validity of categories:

> I am of old and young, of the foolish as much as the wise,
> Regardless of others, ever regardful of others,
> Maternal as well as paternal, a child as well as a man,
> Stuffed with the stuff that is coarse, and stuffed with the stuff
>   that is fine . . .

and a rejection of even the fundamentals of private identity:

> These are the thoughts of all men in all ages and lands, they
>   are not original with me,

> If they are not yours as much as mine they are nothing or next
>   to nothing,
> If they do not enclose everything they are next to nothing . . .

Because of this selflessness, the poet is released from private limitations and is able to speak for nature, democracy, and spirit. He merges with the elements and is no more bound by good and evil, death or birth, reason or insanity than they are. His refutation of the limited self concludes with a transcendence of the "facts" of "reality" in section 23.

The third stage, the "Return to the Divine" (Underhill's illumination), is analogous to Whitman's poem from section 24 to section 33, line 827. Here the spiritual presence joined when one abandons the ego is reexpressed in personality, as all mystical knowledge must be, so that it can be known and felt in the world. This sequence opens by naming the poet for the first time and proceeds to describe the personal self as an object of veneration and wonder. Whitman here reemphasizes his share in all identity and his role as spokesman for spiritual democracy, but he also emphasizes the personal quality of illumination in his defiant celebrations of his physical person ("The scent of these arm-pits is aroma finer than prayer") and his description of the sensual approach to cosmic mystery. His glorification of the body as the bridge to spirit culminates in the well-known apostrophe to touch ("Is this then a touch? . . . . quivering me to a new identity"), and he moves on to another statement of his personal involvement in the miracles of creation and nature (sections 28–32). This phase of the poem is completed as the liberated poet, "afoot" with his "vision," extends himself into time and space in an expansive catalog, which reaches its emotional climax in the remarkable account of a redeemed shipwreck (section 33, lines 818–27). Its final line balances nicely Whitman's mention of his own name at the beginning of the sequence: "I am the man . . . . I suffered . . . . I was there."

The fourth major division of "Song of Myself" corresponds to the mystical dark night of the soul and runs from line 828 in section 33 to line 960 in section 38. It is a sustained treatment of evil and an acknowledgment of the possibility that psychological or supernatural fear can attend the selflessness of mystical experience. Its tone is controlled by two key phrases: "Agonies are one of my changes of garments" (line 840), and "O Christ! My fit is mastering me!" (933). As in classic expressions of the dark night, the poet feels that he is controlled by malevolent forces; he identifies with the hopeless, victimized, and degenerate. Only the description of the battle between the *Bonhomme Richard* and *Serapis* in section 35, which keeps pretty much to the account by John Paul Jones, is at all excepted from the pervasive pessimism of the sequence, and it is immediately modified by section 36, which continues the narrative into the aftermath of the fighting: "The flames spite of all that could be done flickering aloft and below,/ . . . Formless stacks of bodies and bodies by themselves . . . . dabs of flesh upon the masts and spars,/ . . . Black and impassive guns, and litter of powder-parcels, and the strong scent." This infernal imagery and its irrevocability ("These so . . . . these irretrievable") are unusual in Whitman's work and thus disturbing. After his vision of historical suffering, the poet assumes increasingly more degraded identities—the beggar, for instance, or the prisoner "with sweat on my twitching lips." His descent into personal, historical, and cosmic evil reaches its lowest point when he culminates his original radical problem of doubleness and is forced to "look with a separate look on my own crucifixion and bloody crowning!" (960).

The emergence from the dark night of the soul into the unitive state that Patchen calls "Total Identification with the All-Highest" (line 961, section 38 to the end) is explained only by the associative logic of metaphor. Crucifixion necessarily implies resurrection. The poet's triumph follows the inevitable rhythm of the "average unending procession," which continues its evolutionary development despite death. In this sequence he applies mystical knowledge to the problems of the flesh, as he could not in section 5. He has become the new man of unlimited potential, the "friendly and flowing savage," so intimately part of the universal Self that he addresses even the elder gods ("the old cautious hucksters") and nature itself ("Earth! . . . old topknot!") with almost insulting familiarity. He embodies the wisdom of cosmic democracy in order to make it accessible despite the apparitions and restrictions of social identity: "To a drudge of the cottonfields or emptier of privies I lean . . . . on his right cheek I put the family kiss."

Malcolm Cowley thought that these final sections of "Song of Myself" constituted a kind of sermon in which Whitman enunciated the doctrines that control the poem. The description is accurate enough, but the mystical ideas Whitman articulates here are perhaps no more important than his very assumption of the stance of preacher or orator. Now the "Me myself," once so alienated that it withdrew from the social arena, acknowledges the common component of its identity and assumes a number of roles—physician, teacher, priest, guide—by which spirit is realized and expressed in communal work. According to the psychological vocabulary Whitman had not yet formulated, the individual of the opening sequence has become a person in the last.

As the poem ends, the poet prepares to abandon language altogether and become entirely inseparable from the common identity. Entering this ultimate identification and fulfillment, he offers his physical stuff to the single life which is Being, thereby keeping the promise ("every atom belonging to me as good belongs to you") that he made as he loafed in the grass at the beginning of his poem. "I depart as air," he writes at the end, and:

> I effuse my flesh in eddies and drift it in lacy jags.
> I bequeath myself to the dirt to grow from the grass I
>   love,
> If you want me again look for me under your bootsoles.
> You will scarcely know who I am or what I mean,
> But I shall be good health to you nevertheless,
> And filter and fibre your blood.

Although they are found in their least intellectualized or abstracted state in Whitman, American literary structures arising from the mystical process are not uncommon among other writers. *Paterson*, for instance, could be analyzed according to the traditional five stages, and at least one critic has argued that the same principle shapes both the form and meaning of Hart Crane's *The Bridge*.[11] Kenneth Patchen's own rediscovery of the form is closest to his basic impulse in *Memoirs of a Shy Pornographer*, even though that book offers a comic analogue rather than a psychologically realistic description of mystical experience. As a comic fiction and an extended parable, *Memoirs* may be one case in which the form is superimposed on the story, although the divisions between stages do not seem tidy enough to render that anything more than conjecture. I suspect that Patchen's awareness of his use of the mystical form (if he was aware of it) rather grew out of the writing of the book than preceded it.

The first four chapters of *Memoirs of a Shy Pornographer* approximate the first mystical stage, in which the soul is awakened to the search for satisfying love, valid art, and the relationship between them. Albert Budd, who first tells his story in a journal, is so innocent a visionary that he is naive. The source of his moral and artistic authority is his extraordinary creative ability. His imagination is so powerful that he can modify reality. When on a warm May morning he daydreams about below zero weather, "A lot of small boys followed me for blocks—watching me blow steam out on my breath" (14).

Albert's decision to create justice and transcendent love fictionally defines his "Gaining a sense of the Divine." The divine in *Memoirs* is, roughly, the transforming imagination. Inspired by reading and rereading the Perry Mason mystery novels, Albert writes *Spool of Destiny*, a romantic detective story with a heroine named Chaleen—his attempt to resurrect in fiction Chalice Hall, the childhood sweetheart who accidentally drowned. By trying to renew her existence, Albert awakens the critical theme of metaphysical love, especially as love is creativity. He also, as he writes, transforms his own dull routine into something more exciting, a change indicated by his switch as an autobiographer from the journal to a continuous narrative as soon as *Spool of Destiny* is finished.

Authorship, however, is complicated. The book which awakens Budd to a possibility of union in love and art also exposes him to the attacks of a cynical society. Antiliterary themes, which criticize the amoral mercenary element in the literary life, are introduced when unscrupulous agents doctor Albert's book. George Arliss ("the same as an actor") and Skujellifeddy McGranehan pollute his text with asterisks, change his title to *Spill of Desire*, even attempt to turn Chaleen whorish. Their bastardization of

Albert's innocent vision is the first of many examples in *Memoirs* of the inability of the imagination to be self-sufficient.

The literary cocktail society to which Albert is introduced by his agents is equally insensitive. Almost none of the drunken perverts who subject him to alternately funny and frightening social tortures recognizes the worth of the mildly angelic creature in their midst. As the party ends, however, Albert meets Donald Wan, the metaphysical craftsman who has come to take him "home." An inventor, Wan is a creative master of reality, whose great invention can save humanity—if, unlike Albert, he can keep people from misusing it. His relationship with Albert, who can respond creatively to him and his invention, exemplifies the interrelated imaginative activity needed to make reality. But Albert's response alone is not enough. The world is indifferent, even hostile, to the inventor and his altruistic work, and in these first scenes he is already dying of tuberculosis. However, he leads Albert to a large house full of amiable grotesques, where, despite hints of the same troubles that beset the world outside, Budd finds "The First Real Home I Ever Had."

The second mystical phase, the "emptying of Self," is accomplished in the fifth and sixth chapters of *Memoirs*. "My Life as a Private Investigator" records Albert's triumph over the limitations of the strictly individual ego, and in "The Last Party I Ever Went To" he purges his literary identity. Albert's career as a detective, which opens the sequence, is, of course, poignantly bumbling. He has particular trouble with his cheap yellow suit, which soon becomes the symbolic register of his failure as a tough guy. Trying to toss off a drink in the approved *Black Mask* manner, he spills rye whiskey on the jacket, and the moisture draws rust from the useless revolver he attempts to clean. The color and aroma of his clothing make him rather too conspicuous for undercover work, and when commissioned to follow an easily recognizable subject, he manages to shadow the only other green-haired man in New York City. His mistake is part of the general pattern of disguise and confused recognition that begins to dominate the chapter as Albert loses a firm sense of who *he* is, and is unable to trust his memory. His adventures as a detective end when he is fed knockout drops by a client and awakens in a new body.

Budd's journey into a symbolic underworld as part of the identity of a man named Tony establishes the seriousness of *Memoirs of a Shy Pornographer*, and with it the standard against which the comic career of the hero is measured. Although Budd's consciousness is riding Tony's body, he does not succumb entirely to Tony's identity. He cannot understand some of the languages in which Tony is addressed, nor does he approve of Tony's activities as a sort of capitalist gangster. With Tony, Albert travels into a surrealistic landscape, much like Patchen's Dark Kingdom, where the usual limitations of the body are suspended and the institutional malignancy of the familiar world is seen in new, symbolic contexts. Through Tony's eyes Albert views a series of vignettes in which the injustices of modern civilization afflict a symbolic victim, unidentified except that he wears the erstwhile detective's stained yellow suit. These hallucinatory images of society and several almost cabalistic confrontations with sacramental mystery are followed by a scene of religious celebration. Huge throngs gather to listen to a speech denouncing war and affirming life. The chapter ends with a vision of triumph in which Budd is established as the representative of the human spirit:

> And when the morning came a great shout of exultation and thanksgiving arose from every throat. A shy little man in a soiled, lemon-colored suit lifted a photograph high above his head that all might see.
> At once a voice from the highest and farthest hills was heard, and the voice said:
> "Look well upon the face which is before you, my children; for against its gentle wisdom the bondsmen of darkness and evil are as thieves and assassins who would scheme to rob the very wind of its blowing—or who would murder the sun for the heat and the light of the sun!"
> The face was the most beautiful I had ever seen.
> And every face before me there was that face.   (90)

The image of the seeker or saint viewing his own person from outside is similar to Whitman's usage in "Song of Myself" and common in mystical literature as a symbolic expression of the vision that has freed itself from the body. In related applications this schizophrenic image has some currency as a metaphor for insanity, which may or may not be a type of the mystical. At least in his early and middle period Patchen exploits the image to a degree that seems almost compulsive. It appears first in "If We Are to Know Where We Live" from *First Will & Testament*. A man approaches his home to find "them" in control, and he learns their secret:

> They wanted to murder the thing within the house.
> I saw my own face with the knives above it.
> I heard my own screams as they tortured me.
>
> And I was everyone. We all stood there. (84)

The image recurs (I am not attempting to be exhaustive) in "Panel 19" of *Panels for the Walls of Heaven* ("The Builders"), when the protagonist unwittingly acknowledges his death by seeing himself lying unresponsive in bed, and in the visions from *Sleepers Awake* by which Aloysius Best and Almar Gnunsn view each other. It is at perhaps its most dramatic in *The Journal of Albion Moonlight*. The nature of Albion's illumination is suggested by his climactic view of his body:

> *through the gaping aperture Albion had a complete com-
> mand of the room and the party below, being able to look di-
> rectly down at the coffin in which his torn body rested—and,
> as a tear drained from his eye and fell upon the cold face
> which men knew as his own, "Lie still! lie still, you bas-
> tard!" he called down to his corpse. "If you stir, they'll kill
> you!"* (252)

And the fiction ends with Albion seeing his own face "in the blazing windows of all the houses on earth."

Like Albion's, Albert Budd's rapture of doubleness changes him and his story irrevocably. He returns from his psychological journey as if "from the other side of the world," with a new power and toughness beneath his haplessly comic appearance. In the succeeding chapter, an account of another outrageous New York cocktail party, he completes the purging of his old self by shedding the literary identity American society would settle upon him. Between rapes by women inflamed by his book, Budd's narrative consists largely of a mock-heroic catalog of nearly every American poet of reputation and many other cultural celebrities. The ersatz tribute paid these artists associates them with the collection of parasites and phonies at the party. With its ritual exorcism of cultural role and orgiastic culmination, "The Last Party I Ever Went To" concludes Budd's emptying of his worldly self on an appropriately frenetic note.

The third phase of the mystical life, in which the soul returns to its sense of divine mission and experiences illumination, is paralleled in the seventh through the tenth chapter of *Memoirs*. In this sequence Albert reaches the highest fulfillment in love and art that is accessible to human beings and recognizes the cosmic implications of both activities. He is now stronger and more positive than he was before his strange journey; he becomes a teacher and leader. His new adventures begin during an excursion to an idyllic countryside (there is a distinct, almost parodic, dichotomy between the city and the country in *Memoirs*) where he is able to restore the purity of his book and meets Priscilla, who as his beloved is one of the agents of his illumination. That love is creative and respects the same laws that govern art is demonstrated by the need for imaginative agreement between the lovers. When Priscilla equals Albert's act of loving faith, she is able to ignore her lifelong disability and walk.

As the lovers hold hands and make plans, the dying Donald Wan returns to the story. The "inventor to the universe," the chief maker in *Memoirs*, calls Albert back to cooperate in the final creative act by which he attempts to confound all temporal and spatial limitations. Wan's medium this time is a hypodermic needle, and before administering to himself the shot which will transport him to the other world, he gives Albert an injection which makes dream identities real. Albert becomes in succession Perry Mason, a love-in-a-mist, Moby-Dick, and a boxer in the ring with Joe Louis. His sequence of identities is funny and parodic, but it is chiefly important as an example of the extension of self and the community of experience made possible by the creative imagination.

Although love and art triumph during this generally positive period of illumination, we are not permitted to forget that the world is essentially ugly and insensitive. Donald Wan dies pain-fully; raptures between Albert and Priscilla are crudely inter-rupted; Priscilla herself is frequently given to a sort of selfish philistinism. The war is always ominously in the background of the action, and the transcendent powers of the imagination are always limited by the external world, even if they are never limited to it. Against this negative, often dangerous, condition—even because of it—Albert grows in wisdom and power.

The key incident by which Albert develops his prophetic stature occurs in the chapter called "The Deer Are Entering this Beautiful Forest," when he and Priscilla enter a dark wood and are guided to a distinctly churchlike building by an authoritative stranger. As the metaphors suggesting institutional religion grow stronger, the lov-ers are led off by a trinity of young men in white who prepare to murder Priscilla sacrificially in the name of a redeeming afterlife. "Soon you will see beyond the little meanings," they say, and "There is more than just to live—and to die" (162). The scene freezes as the lovers, hypnotized by a traditional rhetoric, prepare to receive death ecstatically. When Albert recalls his priorities, breaks his trance, and routs the assassins, he affirms the principles that no philosophical otherworldliness can justify harming human beings, who are themselves potentially the ultimate divinity, and that concessions to the requirements of a fallen world pervert natural order. He then demonstrates the validity of the innocent perception of unity by establishing a personal relationship with bushes and stars, and calling into the woods an orange-colored waiter with a flaming cart. His efforts convert Priscilla, and the lovers agree to seek permanence for Albert's visionary truths, which they had previously shared only in flashes. The third divi-sion of *Memoirs* ends with their excited plans for elopement.

Albert's dark night of the soul includes the eleventh chapter ("House of the Frowning Heart") and the succeeding "A Radiant Temple Stands Above the Waters" through its fifteenth section (219). In this fourth stage of the mystical way, during which the soul traditionally gives over to despair in separation from the divine goal, Albert is denied both Priscilla and the possibility of any completed creative act. He is ripped from the timeless world he had made of imaginative love and exposed to contemporary life. The sequence opens, appropriately, in New York, where he is again at the mercy of the culture he was able to resist in the country: his novel is again pornographic and he is assaulted by lustful women in a bookstore. As he is rushing to catch a train to Priscilla's country home, he is lured into a mysterious building and held in a maddeningly labyrinthian, but apparently purposeless, captivity until he misses his connection, and with it his chance of meeting Priscilla. The House of the Frowning Heart in which he is trapped is defined only in vague institutional metaphors: religious, economic, familial, medical, literary. Its inhabitants speak exclusively in cliches. Perhaps its most frightening aspect, in the common way of institutions, is that its malevolence is impersonal. Albert is held captive less because he is being restrained than because no one is sufficiently interested to let him go.

In the simplified comic world of *Memoirs* institutions have sanctified human stupidity and numbed the perception of innocence. They inspire and defend all that is evil in human affairs. Their effect upon Albert is seen in the first fifteen sections of "A Radiant Temple Stands Above the Water," in which he returns to the countryside where he left Priscilla. She is dead, and her rural world has, by the loss of Albert's transforming imagination, fallen back into time. Houses are boarded up or destroyed; people have turned savage; the eyes of the young men are "hideous with a new knowledge." Albert is left so dismally lonely and depressed that he is about to despair.

Then he is lifted from his dark night into the unitive stage of mystical growth by Donald Wan's final invention, which was left to him with instructions that he use it only in a time of hopelessness and a warning that its beauty was equaled by its terror. When Albert releases the injection into his arm and by the tubercular inventor's art becomes for a few anachronistic pages an angry Christ whose crucifixion in Times Square is described in a parody of American sportscasting, he enters into an identification with the divine principle that solves the problems and concludes the themes of his book. The heaven he attains in his final chapter is an artifice whereby the imagination is made real. The sky and sun resemble the colored drawings of children, and the heavenly dwellings are like animated children's blocks. Heaven's walls are made up of panels bearing symbolic pictures, most of which are based on the illustrations from the *Splendor Solis* of Solomon Trismosin.[12] The strange visions of the sixteenth-century spiritual alchemist are, again, images of the transfiguration of matter affected in art by the inspired imagination.

The whimsical setting makes Albert's heaven a child's dream; its other characteristics also respect the reduced scale of comic writing. As an analogue for the mystical condition of union, it satisfies Albert's simple desires. Priscilla is there, with Albert's son, whom she died bearing. Donald Wan is there, with his community of lovable eccentrics. Chaleen (Chalice) Hall is there, even though she inspires an outburst of the jealousy that did not entirely die with Priscilla's body. All in all, it is a place where innocent love thrives and people can live in peace with the wonderful creations of their imaginations. It is a state of being from which one can start without hindrance to discover God or to probe to the source of the mystery. In other words, heaven is one's birthright for this world, even though we are not permitted to forget that it exists here only as artifice: the book ends when Albert returns to earth and converses about life and death with the unidentified man he looks for on Patchin Place. Reality and art, however, are not necessarily antithetical terms in this fiction, and Albert's triumph, although comic, is also transcendent. As he "flies right up out" of his book, not knowing how else to end it, he may remind us for a moment of the exhilarating departure of his great ancestor, who soared out of "Song of Myself" "as air."

Patchen's use of traditional mystical structure in *Memoirs* relies on the special circumstances created by comic characterization and the playful use of allegory. He never attempted to repeat his success with it or to develop again so much paraphrasable intellectual content. Instead, he continued to search out new forms for visionary perception and to discover limiting principles to intensify and guide his emotional weapon. In the years after he abandoned long prose fiction, he became increasingly interested in spatially limited forms. With them he attempted to escape the rigid logic of time, which clearly bothered him in his most ambitious books. The organization of material in space rather than temporal sequence is, of course, most important in the poem-paintings, but it is also clearly at work in some of the *Panels for the Walls of Heaven*, for instance, or in those later lyrics which are fitted to the page. Spatial consistency also characterizes much of the abundant experimentation of the fifties, when Patchen wrote groups of poems in a more or less similar shape, then abandoned it to move on to another. The prose-poems of *The Famous Boating Party*, the variations of the limerick in *Hurrah for Anything*, and the modified ballad forms of *When We Were Here Together* are examples.

This experimentation seeks the limiting form that insures unity, but also the liberating form that releases the poem to its natural shape. Especially in his later years, Patchen appears to feel a need for structures to which he can return without violating the organic imperative. Recurrence and predictability are, after all, principles as natural as spontaneity and intuition. William Carlos Williams believed that he had solved the problem with the development of his variable foot, and Patchen sought similar combinations of freedom and law. One of his discoveries is form based on word count—the pattern, for instance, of the lyrics which made up *Orchards, Thrones & Caravans* and were later collected in *When We Were Here Together*. As Frederick Eckman pointed out, each of these poems has a three-word title, is broken into a regular stanzaic pattern according to the number of lines (4-1-4-1-7-1), and has a consistent number of words for each line (5-4-3-5 in the first stanza, and so forth).[13] Each poem contains seventy words in all.

Patchen adjusts this form to a remarkable range of themes and emotions. His lyrics run from fantasies for children ("The Magical Mouse"), to painful evocations of human mortality ("Lowellville Cemetery: Twilight"), to love poems, to celebrations of natural splendor, to comic sketches written in a grotesque parody of dialect ("Little Cannibal's Bedtimesong"). The word count gives him stable relationships within the poem, upon which he can vary syllable length or number, or, occasionally, metric structure. He avoids syntactical repetition by varying between the end-stopped line, the stanza, or the entire poem itself as grammatical unit. His juxtaposition of short and long lines can be used either for emphasis or to hurry past relatively unimportant pronouns. Although the poems are similar in structure, the form does not trigger the memory, as does, for instance, the rhyme scheme of the traditional sonnet, which has its own sound and its own aesthetic satisfaction. We become accustomed to the overall pattern, the way each poem ("The Constant Bridegrooms" for instance) starts off purposefully:

> Far down the purple wood
> Coats of a company
> Of silent soldiers
> Flap idly in the wind

has its continuity broken and its pace slowed across the eccentric stanzaic arrangement of the inner poem:

> There they have stood
>
> Since early day
> Faces turned incuriously to the sound
> Of the dry rustling
> Of leaves in the wind
>
> No command has reached

and then picks up momentum across the longer fifth stanza:

> Them there
> All silent have they stood
> As
> Though they were asleep
> Now night darkens their coats
> Far away
> Their names are spoken

which leads into an aphoristic final line:

> Somewhere at world's end.

But this process never becomes so fixed that we can anticipate it exactly. Patchen may have felt, however, that the form was too limiting. He doesn't seem able to use it as a vehicle for his great energy or to release his prophetic denunciations. It works best for delicacy or whimsy, and Patchen does not strain to fit it to his larger schemes. Instead, he develops other new forms.

If Frederick Eckman is correct that the word-count form of *When We Were Here Together* is a sonnet variation, then *Poemscapes*, which followed it, might profitably be considered Patchen's reworking of the sonnet sequence. It is written in many forms, each with its own integrity, which modify and complement each other, and combine, finally, into a major poem, the form of which imitates the mind and emotion of Kenneth Patchen. The book is made up of forty-two individual poemscapes, prose-poems which, as their name implies, are spatially limited. A poemscape fits a page precisely and is divided into four separately titled sections which are consistent in physical size from poem to poem. The sections themselves have three-word titles, are distinct entities, and are numbered consecutively through the book, which contains 168 in all. Each poemscape has 140 words, the first section having 36, the second 54, the third 14, and the last 36 (the count of individual sections will vary by as many as 3 words). In poemscapes which develop a single theme, the relationship of statement to demonstration grows naturally out of the juxtaposition of duration. The first section states the theme; the second elaborates upon it, sometimes with philosophical directness; the third repeats the implications of the theme in an epigrammatic image; and the fourth section summarizes and applies the statement evolved. This fundamental argument is illustrated more clearly than is typical in Poemscape XXX, which draws various thematic and narrative strains together into one of the strongest statements of principle in the book:

117) GOLDEN PLUM BUDS
We imagine one another so badly. We confuse one
another with appearances that form in chairs and ocean-
liners and with being some longago-Greek or "young girl
walking across field at sevenpm April3rd" or being "my-
keeper'sbrother."

GOLDEN PLUM BUDS (118
Whatever we imagine for one another is wrong to the
extent that we separate a state of being from its does-
ness. Because all appearances have a common origin in
the unseeable fluidity *which issues forth from the action
of its own flowing*. Existence is verb (No "objects,"
no "things-to-be-named"—*doing itself does itself do*.)

119) MY INNOCENT COMPANIONS
They imagine an earth, a sky; imagine that they
are alive: and they die.

FRIEND THE RABBIT (120
He imagines himself a bird with long ears, ball-y
tail, chassis lovingly covered with soft golden fur.
At sea a fortnight he sights a ship, but everybody
a-bored pretends to see only a flying rabbit.

Although Poemscape XXX is unusually coherent and unified
according to its own vocabulary and development, each of its
sections is also part of a book-long sequence which reappears from
time to time under its own title. We are kept informed, for in-
stance, of the adventures of "My Innocent Companions" through-
out *Poemscapes*, and their appearance here not only adds to Patch-
en's discussion of the imagination and relates it to earlier
descriptions of human faculties; it also continues our interest in the
frequently zany activities of the characters who represent an aspect
of innocence. Patchen uses many such sustained subtopics to
isolate strands of his thought and observation. Then he inter-
weaves them. The complex allusive surface that results suggests
the expansive liveliness of the awakened perception. In any par-
ticular poemscape these self-contained thematic sequences can
either complement the main idea, as "My Innocent Companions"

does in XXX, or develop tensions between themes. Many comic or romantic poemscapes are interrupted by "The Little Essays," a series of philosophical statements, or "Night Letter," one of the important strains of protest. By particular applications of these thematic elements, which make their definitive statement outside of any single poemscape, Patchen is able to balance his often uncompromising statements and respect the complexity of his responses. He can speak of love, for example, in his familiar romantic language—"And now it is your grace that I would celebrate, O my flowering one"—but he is not limited to it. The flippant wisdom of one of the "Kindness of Clowns" sequence gives us an entirely different sense of the toughness and durability of human love: "Suspicion made the first pairapants; but, Joey, it'll be love'll take off the last."

This elaborate system of reference between the larger and smaller patterns growing out of *Poemscapes* rewards the sympathetic reader with several kinds of understanding. Each poemscape can be read separately, but it is made richer by knowledge of its context. Each is its own form, but also part of many other forms, extensive or local, in various stages of development. Each is self-contained, but also leads off in innumerable directions. Together they become a single heroic poem which cannot be paraphrased, written in a form that is without precedent. The book clearly has a beginning and an ending: it opens with a celebration of natural wonder entitled "Fashioned In Love," and concludes by echoing that first title—implying, obviously, that the poem has come full cycle. But the internal development of consciousness cannot be so easily isolated, and the overall form of *Poemscapes*, its unity, can be defined only in terms of its own existence. It is probably Patchen's most technically perfect work, a persuasive memorial of the formal inventiveness which distinguished his career after he discovered his personal idiom in *First Will & Testament*.

Chapter 6

After Antiliterature:

Patchen's Poetics

*The poetic quality is not marshalled in rhyme or uniformity
or abstract addresses to things nor in melancholy complaints
or good precepts, but is the life of these and much else and is
in the soul:*

—Whitman, Preface (1855)

In a rare statement about poetics, Kenneth Patchen once observed that "a great many people have forgotten that the way to build a house is to build it. Those who work with their hands know that the proper method for moving a heavy stone is to get a good firm hold, brace your feet, kick it into motion with the nubs of your fists, and ride it to where you want it to go." The remark illustrates his refusal to distinguish between the methodology and the act of creativity. It also expresses the attitude he shares with most exponents of organic poetry, that the poem is its own prime mover, and the poet the agent through whom it emerges from the undifferentiated source and takes direction. Unlike many modern poets, then, Patchen developed no extensive theory of versification and refused to discuss the composition of his poems. His reluctance to explicate was complicated and reinforced by his insistence that the poem is inseparable from the needs and character of its author. Elsewhere in his statement, Patchen asserted that "Hart Crane's *Bridge* failed because he didn't think enough about its structure as it had to do with his own *structure as a man*."[1] Faced with Patchen's strategic retreat into the mysteries of first causes, we cannot always identify precisely the working poetic laws to which specific techniques conform. If we want to understand him fully we must attempt to re-create his implicit concept of the craft of poetry almost as we would compose a fiction. Because of the obliquity of the effort, we can probably hope only to cultivate a distant kinship to *Alice in Wonderland*, which one of Damon Runyon's gangsters described as "nothing but a pack of lies, but very interesting in spots."

The aspirations of Patchen's verse are, of course, essentially personalistic, its methods essentially organic. He seeks illuminations of, and access to, some universalized identity through the particulars of individual experience, and the theory of organic literature, as it proceeds from Emerson and Whitman, provides him with all the theory he needs. As an artist, he is obliged to seek a new language and a new technique for each rediscovery of the unity of things, must in a sense reoriginate his entire poetic each time he *re-cognizes* the presence of the mystery beneath the appearances of the world. It is morally as well as artistically imperative that he respond to the challenges of reality with sufficient technical resources to respect its integrity as well as his own.

To such demands Patchen brings a variety of prosodic skills. He ranges from regularly rhymed poems written in analyzable metric patterns to prose-poems and other extreme forms of open verse. Rhymed and counted poems are the least characteristic and technically the least interesting of his writings, but it is worth noting that he did not become so embroiled in ideological quarrels about the priorities of free and accentual-syllabic verse that he rejected any poetic tools out of hand. Early in his career he used a rhyming metric line chiefly in the doggerel satire, a genre he soon abandoned, and in the archaically formal love poems, doubtless made in lieu of many ornaments, which he addressed to Miriam, his wife. Later he used rhyme, usually for local effect rather than as the pattern of an entire poem, in some of the formal experiments of *Orchards, Thrones & Caravans* and such quiet lyrics as "Wide, Wide in the Rose's Side." He exploited the device energetically and ingeniously, but often self-consciously, so that it worked best for thematic emphasis or as an expression of whimsy. In complex or discursive poems—"An Old Pair of Shoes" from *When We Were Here Together*, for instance—it could become heavy-handed.

Whatever the success or failure of his counted prosody, the bulk of Patchen's work is in open forms—what for lack of better terms we call free verse—and it is upon his achievement in this idiom that our judgment of him must ultimately rest. The situation has posed another difficulty for a discussion of Patchen's poetics, because we have not had a critical vocabulary for open forms comparable in sophistication and exhaustiveness to that developed for traditional verse,[2] not even one (as we had from William Carlos Williams, for instance) of Patchen's own making. Despite more recent efforts by some of his allies, Patchen's contemporary reputation was largely established during the era when the new criticism, with its reliance on the intellectual model of seventeenth-century metaphysical wit, was in the ascendant, and its analytic method was radically inapplicable to Whitman and his successors. But, as Richard Chase noted in *Walt Whitman Reconsidered*, it was just such "highly skilled linguistic and symbolistic criticism" that was used to approach Whitman, with the predictable result that he and his work were misvalued.[3] The same has been true of Patchen, as for years it was of such maverick poets as William Carlos Williams and the radically visionary Robert Duncan, who is just emerging from relative anonymity in the fifth decade of his distinguished career.[4]

Traditional critical and prosodic notations are often inadequate to even the first approaches to open forms. In most traditional verse, for instance, the line is the basic unit which gathers individual sounds and establishes the rhythmic pattern of the poem. In free verse, however, the unit of rhythmic sound may be the line, as in Whitman's poetry, or it may be stanzaic—that is, in short poems the modulation of sound may cross over line divisions and become a recognizable pattern only in the completion of the stanza. Or it may even be the entire poem itself. William Carlos Williams's poems, especially the shortest, are often based upon the completion, rather than the repetition, of a single rhythmic unit. "The Locust Tree in Flower" is an example.

Patchen's own contribution to the poetry of a single rhythm is a jeu d'esprit which may also have been meant to offend officious readers. "The Murder of Two Men by a Young Kid Wearing Lemon-colored Gloves" consists simply of the word "Wait" arranged in various combinations around the page and building to a climax in the only other word in the poem, "Now." This bit of visual wordplay is first a joke, of course, but it is also a kind of skeletal exhibition of some of Patchen's other concerns. It is a poem, for instance, in which the poet provides a title and the outline of emotional development and the reader is asked to perform an essential act of imagination.[5] It is also an extended instruction on how to read a poem in time, how to keep the developing rhythm in one's head as the poet leads to the fulfillment of both sound and meaning. Although it is an exaggerated example of Patchen's use of extended rhythmic units, it points up his attention to the possibility of writing poems that are completely integrated movements of sound. That the pace of the sound is to a large degree determined by the movement of the eye on the page is significant even at this relatively early (1943) stage in his career. Patchen almost never uses a ready-made line, because the division of a poem into distinct rhythmic units would violate its organic qualities. In Denise Levertov's words, "in organic poetry the peculiar rhythms of the parts are in some degree modified, if necessary, in order to discover the rhythm of the whole."[6]

Whether or not its rhythmic authority is to be modified, the line remains the primary structural unit on which the solidity of a poem depends. In his open forms, Patchen uses both a metric line and a free, or phrasal line. This latter is the familiar line of most American free verse; its stress and duration are built upon the natural grouping of words in speech. Patchen uses the metric line only infrequently: for formality or for occasional local effect in free forms based otherwise on the phrasal line, where meter interrupts or supplements the reader's sense of continuity. In "My Generation Reading the Newspapers," for instance, the theme of revolutionary revenge is built by phrasal lines to an emotional conclusion, which is abruptly stated in two lines of nearly regular iambic pentameter:[7]

> I mean no/thing short/ of blood/ in eve/ry street
> on earth/ can fit/ly voice/ the loss/ of these.

Not only does the suddenly insistent rhythm intensify the emotion of the lines, it continues across the line ending, following the syntax and extending the time of emotional reaction. Especially because of the caesura after "earth," the first foot of the second line is actually read as a sixth foot for the first line. It becomes a final emphatic addition to a statement that had already seemed complete, and it deepens the tone of deliberated rage which gives the poem its power.

Patchen's free line falls naturally into several rough categories. He sometimes uses a parallelism similar to Walt Whitman's, in which lines possess identical syntactical structures and each line picks up and adds to the statement made in the line preceding. As Whitman does in such characteristic passages as the opening sentence of "Out of the Cradle Endlessly Rocking," Patchen usually uses parallelism in a series of adverbial phrases that set the condition for the action of the poem:

> In the shape of this night, in the still fall
> of snow, Father
> In all that is cold and tiny, these little birds
> and children
> In everything that moves tonight, the trolleys
> and the lovers, Father
> In the great hush of country, in the ugly noise
> of our cities
>
> "At the New Year"

Pure parallelism is relatively uncommon in Patchen's work and it never becomes more than an occasional and subordinate structural principle. There is, however, a line structure based upon a similar, although less sophisticated, repetition of syntax, to which Patchen returns with some frequency. At its simplest, this line is defined by repeating a word or verbal formula (rather than a complete syntactical structure), and the repetition establishes a crude beat for the rhythm of the poem. Unsuitable for rhythmic delicacy, it works best when the poet wants a coercive emphasis—as does, for instance, Allen Ginsberg in Part III of his "Howl." Each of his nineteen lines is based on the statement "I'm with you in Rockland," and then extended each to its own length according to a prosody probably analogous (if the comparison is not pressed) to jazz improvisation. Patchen's own use of this somewhat mechanical device characteristically elaborates an emotional statement developed in other kinds of versification. In "The Hangman's Great Hands," for example, a rudimentary parallelism is induced when the speaker momentarily abandons his narrative for a repeated statement of his emotion. His return to a definitive adjective establishes a base for each line and the regularity of a rhythmic pattern, which is brought to climax by an unexpected run-on. The repetition also sets the context for a series of explanations that emphasize his prophetic rage:

> Somehow the cop will sleep tonight, will make love
> to his wife. . .
> *Anger won't help. I was born angry.*
> *Angry that my father was being burnt alive in the mills;*
> *Angry that none of us knew anything but filth and poverty.*
> *Angry because I was that very one somebody was supposed*
> *To be fighting for*

The most primitive of Patchen's other syntactically determined line units simply lists thoughts one to a line and is used primarily in a sort of disjointed monologue:

> What should they care about?
> It's quaint.
> Twelve kids on a fire escape . . .
> Flowers on the windowsill . . .
> You're damn right.
> That's the way it is.
> That's just the way it is.
>
> "The Slums"

A related, but more sophisticated syntactical usage is found in the line (sometimes sustained throughout a poem) in which line endings correspond to and reinforce syntactical divisions. It is, of course, a short line, but it extends the time needed to make a complete statement, which thus acquires deliberation and weight:

> The air must be kind
> To the clouds and stars
> That they never
> Cry out

> Or tear their lives away
> From Thee
> As we do
> And have done
>   "How Silent Are the Things of Heaven"

Both kinds of abrupt syntactical line are, again, used more often for local effects than as the definition of an overall pattern.

"The Slums," however, illustrates the problem of ellipsis that is to be found to some extent in all syntactically dominated forms. Much free verse is written in a sort of poetic shorthand by which line divisions and other pauses in sound replace some connective grammar. The reader is asked to fill in by grasping the basic situation of the poem. Usually there is no problem involved in such incomplete syntax. In Part 1 of "Howl," for instance, Allen Ginsberg begins a declarative sentence that extends into a series of relative clauses so long that it outlasts syntactical memory. The sentence is in fact completed at the end of Part 1, but grammatical closure is essentially irrelevant to understanding it. Long before the end, the reader has accepted the convention that each relative clause is a variation on the theme of madness, and has no difficulty in applying it to the rest of the poem. In more tightly organized poems, however, syntactical shorthand can create ambiguities—as it does in one of the best poems from *Before the Brave*, "Let Us Have Madness Openly":

> Let us have madness openly, O men
> Of my generation. Let us follow
> The footsteps of this slaughtered age:
>
> .   .   .   .
> With the face that dead things wear—
>   nor ever say
>
> We wanted more; we looked to find
> An open door, an utter deed of love . . .

The "nor" at the end of the first stanza has no negative antecedent. Its precise application is obscure, and it could be taken to deny the positive statement in the second stanza—which the poet obviously means to affirm.

Another of Patchen's free lines might be called the cumulative line. It is a grammatically end-stopped rhythmic unit, but one which develops a kind of emotional crescendo, usually by lengthening (or, rarely, by decreasing) each line in relation to the last so that the length of the line supposedly corresponds to its thematic weight. The gradual lengthening of sound attempts to build an almost unbearable tension, which is broken by an abrupt return to a short line, so that the accumulated emotion may be released. Walt Whitman uses the cumulative line with a remarkable balance of delicacy and power in the fifth and sixth sections of "When Lilacs Last in the Dooryard Bloom'd," in which he describes the progress of Abraham Lincoln's funeral train, with its attendant evocation and draining of emotion, from station to station on its journey west. That is the lesson of the master. Allen Ginsberg, again, offers a clearer, because less sophisticated, example. The principle of operation of the cumulative line can be isolated in Part 4 of "Kaddish":

> with your eyes
> with your eyes of Russia
> with your eyes of no money
> with your eyes of false China
> with your eyes of Aunt Elanor
> with your eyes of starving India

and so forth until the duration of the line reaches "with your eyes of the killer Grandma you see on the horizon from the Fire-Escape," and then begins a decrescendo of progressively shorter units.

As Ginsberg uses the cumulative line, it is highly artificial, and physical considerations can easily force the choice of language. Patchen's line is more subtle, and he often integrates it more successfully into the total sound of a poem. He uses it, for instance, to describe growing sexual excitement in "And What With the Blunders":

> a closing of eyes
> and falling unfalteringly
> over a warm pure country and something
>   crying

but in short groups whose tendency to crescendo is restrained by an insistent return to noncumulative rhythmic units.

Thus far I have described secondary usage. Patchen's primary line, which informs his work of all kinds and periods, is grouped roughly according to stressed phrases so that each line has an approximately equivalent duration and is characterized by heavy use of enjambment. Its rhythm is determined by ear rather than by measure, and the weight of each line (at least ideally) is adjusted to the demands of the entire poem. Patchen hints at his understanding of line when he says: "I am not sure but that our whole conception of the verse-line is wrong. Words have distinct values of relationship that have no bearing whatever on the relationship of line to line; if this is remembered, of course, we get a perfect relationship of line to line *over the whole poem*. There is such a thing as weight in words. A rhythm felt is a rhythm that has its own laws. It is an absolute mistake to ladle out stress like a cook measuring off the ingredients for a cake."[8]

Patchen's theory (if it can be called that) is exemplified in his sturdily compressed verse. His line can be as short as the one or two phrasal units of "The Figure Motioned with its Mangled Hand":

> It was rumored/on the block
> Ethel/is going to let go tonight.
> I made big about it,/strutting
> Down 5th/eyeing the babies over,
> Thinking they look like mudhens
> Next to my/little piece of tail.

Or it can be as long as the three- to five-unit line of "He Was Alone (as in Reality) upon His Humble Bed":

> I sat down/and said beer/thinking Scotch/and there by God
> Was my woman/just as I/had always known/she would be
> And I went over to her/and she said/come home with me
>
> .   .   .   .
>
> I was wanting it then/but she said/some more things/and
>   started
> To cry/and I slammed on my coat/and said/you lousy bitch/
>   which shut
> Her up/and I put my key/in the lock

The length of a line in time, of course, does not depend upon the number of its phrasal groups, because the groups themselves have no set temporal value. They rather mark the rhythm of a line, its recurrence of stress. The two-group line of "The Figure Motioned" is shorter than most of Patchen's two-group lines, and the four-group line of "He Was Alone" is longer than other four-group lines. Under certain circumstances, a two-group line can actually be longer than a three-group line, or it can be equal to it. In fact, Patchen's verse probably falls most commonly into a natural balance between lines of two and three groups:

> The innocent alone/approach evil
> Without fear;/in their appointed flame
> They acknowledge/all living things.
> The only evil/is doubt;/the only good
> Is not death,/but life./To be is to love.
> This I thought/as I stood/while the snow
> Fell/in that bitter place,/and the riders
> Rode their motionless sleds/into a nowhere
> Of sleep. . . .
>
> "The Rites of Darkness"

The duration of each line varies according to the line's weight in the overall movement of the poem. As far as I can tell, this temporal factor is determined by the poet's subjective sense of his work, and is accessible only to description and not to analysis.

Patchen's enjambment is also in evidence here. In the third and fourth lines of "The Figure Motioned," for instance, we struggle against versification to read "strutting/Down 5th" as an uninterrupted phrase. This tension between syntactical and prosodic entities helps to pack the line, and is one of the devices by which Patchen adds weight or dignity to his statement. His intuitive feeling for rhythm is rarely mistaken, and he is also often able to focus attention on an important theme by abruptly adjusting the sound in which it is perceived—by interrupting the pattern of line length:

> I doubt that any two lives touch except as they go
> back

> Into the darkness,
> Or come all the way out into the light.
>
> "Hovenweep"

or by establishing a pattern of contrasting line lengths over an entire poem. He frequently switches line forms in order to isolate and develop a particular theme. In "Thinking Rock," for example, he suddenly breaks the movement of his basic line in favor of the simple syntactical unit in which line endings correspond to grammatical pauses. The change speeds up the sound of the verse and marks the division between background and situation:

> Not only men, but the waters, and the forest,
> Have souls; morning, the darkness, rain,
> Bear cubs, fog, and the wind: have souls;
> And these, too, the rock thinks well of.
> Beautifully,
> And on the rock sits
> The pretty Colleen.
> About her head so fair and small
> The white eyes of the air whirl
> In happy solitude.

Patchen's characteristically strong stanza grows naturally from the phrasal line. It is a burly poetic unit that is rarely of fixed length, but is assigned whatever number of lines best agrees with its weight in the total poem. Its solidity results from an interaction of Patchen's strengths of both sound and syntax. He normally uses straightforward declarative sentences in conjunction with the phrasal line and its enjambment. The overlapping of lines, often by short syntactical units, reinforces the corners of the verse as metal elbows reinforce the corners of a packing crate—with the effect that the verse and its meaning seem compressed. The process is demonstrated in Patchen's recreation of a father's brooding over the loss of his daughter. Forced to balance the sense against sound, the reader sensually perceives something of the restraint by which the father controls his emotion:

> is it like this,
> Dying? Just the moment going over

> The edge of body, nothing left there
> That grass cannot solve?
>
> "Peter's Diary in Goodentown"

Patchen occasionally varies this basic stanza by making no important use of enjambment. Syntactical and rhythmic pauses are here mutually reinforcing. This stanza reads, of course, with greater fluidity than the deliberately interrupted stanza Patchen commonly uses, and in general terms is perhaps more appropriate to the representation of inevitability than to the expression of conflict. Compare to the passage from "Peter's Diary in Goodentown" the description of death in "Of the Same Beauty Were Stars Made":

> Of the same beauty ‖ were stars made
> That they might guide ‖ their earthly sister
> When she undertook ‖ the white still journey
> Into the country ‖ of His gentle keeping.

The feeling of peaceful fulfillment in this little poem about the cosmic unity of life arises not only from the unusually regular two-beat, seven-word line, and the markedly stronger caesura (as I have indicated) than Patchen normally employs, but also from some subtle manipulations of patterns of sound. In the first two and one-half lines, the sentence structure is directly progressive. Adjectives are not stressed; verbs are. The smoothness of syntactical flow is enhanced by the verbal regularity that finds four words in the first rhythmic unit and three in the second in each of the first two lines. In the third line, however, the word grouping is inverted, and the second group introduces a slight irregularity by placing two modifiers before "journey"—interfering with the directness of statement as well as with the rhythm. Because of the barely noticeable double stress drawn by the adjectives, the poem marks time, becomes for the moment asymmetrical, and reaches a kind of preclimactic tension. The sensation of waiting induced by the break in the verbal pattern is resolved by the mild assonance between "journey" and "country," a similarity in sound reinforced by the caesura in the fourth line. In the silence created by the combination of the partial rhyme and the pause in linear continuity, the final phrase, toward which the entire weight of the sentence is carried, completes the syntactical unit even as it explains the logic of the poem.

Patchen's other stanzas are usually based on the various kinds of line already described—the cumulative line, for instance, in which the stanzaic unit is simply the entire development of a single progressive rhythm. However, they need not be particularly bulky. A stanza can be as short as one line, if Patchen feels that by isolating the line he will give it a desirable temporal context. He is intensely conscious of the time and pace of his poems, and he frequently uses the blank spaces on a page to slow the reader down. "What Is the Beautiful?" is an example. After each stanza of this poem Patchen instructs us to "Pause"; each new stanza then opens, "And begin again."[9]

In addition to such extensions of his basic free-verse lines, Patchen uses a number of more patterned stanzas. Particularly in his later collection, *When We Were Here Together*, and, to a lesser extent, in *Red Wine & Yellow Hair*, he sets many of his whimsical protest songs into something resembling a traditional lyric quatrain and tries a few imitations of the English folk ballad. These late experiments with established form probably grew out of the stanza divided to accommodate a refrain, which had always been one of Patchen's more ambitious structural units. Usually his refrain completes and restates the meaning of the entire stanza:

> Take the useful events
> For your tall.
> Red mouth.
> Blue weather.
> To hell with power and hate and war.
>
> .   .   .   .
>
> Tell God that we like
> The rain, and snow, and flowers,
> And trees, and all things gentle and clean
> That have growth on the earth.
> White winds.
> Golden fields.
> To hell with power and hate and war.
>
> "Instructions for Angels"

The long refrain line here also picks up and completes a cumulative development of sound.

Finally, Patchen sometimes uses free-verse stanzas of a fixed number of lines. The most common is the two-line stanza in which he attempts to combine the aphoristic economy of the couplet with the open-endedness of the phrasal line. Although there is an occasional overlapping of syntax across stanzas, inducing another kind of counterpoint between sound and meaning, this two-line form is characteristically closed, so that the poem builds on relatively distinct statements, which are isolated in time and brought together in the final couplet (see "The Fox" for an example). This is by far the most strictly defined of the verse forms to which Patchen regularly returns.

These many forms of line and stanza permit Patchen considerable flexibility in his response to experience. To the possibilities they permit him he brings an equally extensive vocabulary—one that is again, for better or for worse, unmistakably his own. His poetic language ranges from transcriptions of American speech, often in a slangy working-stiff idiom, to a slightly elevated vocabulary based generally in theology, to the stiffly poeticized usage of some of the traditional love lyrics. These three poetic dictions might represent Patchen's versions of the plain, middle, and high style of traditional rhetoric. The high style can in effect be dismissed without discussion. Patchen uses it only in presentation pieces for his wife, and although he has written some surprisingly fresh poems in this mode, his adaptations of it often become overpoweringly sentimental.

Patchen's transcriptions of contemporary speech are more ambitious and closer to the basic values of his art. Especially in the early books, he often attempts to uncover the poetry inherent in such unadorned popular usage as:

> Understand that they were sitting just inside the door
> At a little table with two full beers and two empties.
> There were a few dozen people moving around, killing
> Time and getting tight because nothing meant anything
> Anymore

As these lines from "The State of the Nation" suggest, Patchen's colloquial style is characterized by simple grammatical structures, which rely heavily on the basic subject-predicate relationship. There are relatively few modifiers, and those usually more for the purpose of information than for the creation of a new concept. Relative clauses, when they occur at all, do not interrupt the purposeful movement of the sentence. The elliptical syntax of oral usage is imitated in the introductory imperative "Understand"; and the passage represents also something of the vagueness that creeps into speech which is supported by either gesture or the context of intimate conversation ("nothing meant anything anymore"). Grammatical usage is loose, even lazy, and ultimately falls back on what is most familiar, such as the formulaic imagery ("killing time and getting tight") that has become part of American slang.

In "The State of the Nation" unadorned everyday speech mirrors the flatness of the saloon life described and the irrelevance in world culture of the national life it represents. But such noncommittal language can also be applied to normally exciting circumstances and stress disparities between the verbal and emotional structures of the poem. Much of the terror of "Death Will Amuse Them" arises from the juxtaposition of a murderous divine whim with the informative conversational language in which it is explained.

Patchen's thematic applications of his plain style are interesting but secondary. He uses popular speech largely for its intrinsic poetry. At its best it is a vigorous language, and when Patchen makes full use of the slang for which he has a good ear, it is a colorful one. In his slanging poems he often assumes the roles of tough guy or hipster. The latter is the perennial American character who is so absorbed in the popular culture of the moment that he is unable to think in anything but the most baroque slang, and whose talk is full of slang cliches—"I told her what to do and we did it, Jesus I said, is your name McCoy?" ("Eve of St. Agony"). From this vantage point Patchen simply emits a flow of hard-core colloquialism, almost as if he were purging himself of his years of American culture:

> she's like you like her, now don't you try to spike her,
> she's the nuts, she's a mile of Camel butts,
> she's honey in the money, she's my pearl
>> "A Letter on the Use of Machine Guns at Weddings"

The slanging often becomes so furious that Patchen's cliches emerge garbled or assume strange juxtaposition. A kind of gallows dance of American folk wisdom results:

> Later I went in for stripteasing before Save Democracy Clubs;
> When the joint was raided we were all caught with our pants
> down.
> But I will say this: I like butter on both sides of my bread
> And my sister can rape a Hun any time she's a mind to
>> "Eve of St. Agony"

Although Patchen emphasizes the unpoetic, his use of colloquialism is not so unselective as he makes it appear. He uses everyday language economically and exploits both its strength and its capacity for surprises. In "Street Corner College," for instance, the coldly bitter complaint about the hopelessness of a generation of urban youth is made in an unexceptional but effective language which draws largely on the strength of direct statement:

> Betting on slow horses; drinking cheap gin.
> We have nothing to do; nowhere to go; nobody.
> Last year was a year ago; nothing more.
> We weren't younger then, nor older now.

This almost frighteningly plain speech drives the poem mercilessly into the psychological emptiness of America's victims (who "shall probably not be quite dead when we die"), and carries a social protest of considerable harshness. In the first lines of the final stanza, however, Patchen varies his language slightly in order to hint at spiritual as well as social alienation. Without breaking the continuity of diction, he suggests the inevitability of the more than merely sociological void awaiting his characters:

> We are the insulted, brother, the desolate boys.
> Sleepwalkers in a dark and terrible land,
> Where solitude is a dirty knife at our throats.

The use of the abstracted adjective as noun in the first line, the metaphors in the second and third, and the paired modifiers in line two: these verbal sophistications appear here for the first time in the poem. They make the situation universal even as they render it more intense, and their implications are confirmed in the final lines:

> Cold stars watch us, chum,
> Cold stars and the whores.

"Street Corner College" illustrates the art in general of Patchen's plain style. Abstractions are avoided. The vocabulary is exact and rooted in familiar things. Poetic excitement grows not out of any connotative richness of sound, but out of the struggle of language to strip away illusions and expose the reader to something of the meanness of the human condition. Grounded in the commonplace and tawdry, Patchen's plain style discovers its own imaginative freedom and invents its own uniquely illuminating imagery. Something of the grimly fundamental world view resulting from environmental oppression is suggested when Patchen takes metaphors from the reductive personification of street slang —as "the ass of dark" ("The Queer Client"). And he admires the human impulse to dredge new perceptions out of even the ugliest experience. The protagonist of "Biography of Southern Rain," for instance, observes that "rain, like memory, can come in filthy clothes."

Patchen's middle style, his psycho-theological vocabulary, is based upon a perception of reality that is less immediately mundane. His syntactical unit in this more openly transcendent mode is often complex and extended, and makes heavy use of relative clauses. His nouns are now frequently exotic and they often name symbolic qualities (light, darkness, being, etc.) rather than specific objects. Modifiers are used liberally. Usually they transform a noun or verb rather than identify its application with greater precision.

Patchen's transcendental vocabulary can be seen working in relatively subdued fashion in "Of the Same Beauty Were Stars Made" (see p. 116), which is not nearly so complex as many of his other cosmic poems. To the theme that all things live one life—

which is the central theme of this middle range—he applies, first, a semitheological vocabulary that takes its meaning from the sacramental context established in the final line. The religious connotations of "guide," "sister," and "journey," the concepts of star-substance and divine country, and the feeling of intimate illumination in the paired adjectives of the third line are all typical of Patchen's willingness to draw upon the emotion stored in the language of orthodoxy and compare his own vision of union to the more familiar concept of religious salvation.

The use of the gerund at the end of "Of the Same Beauty" is also characteristic. Patchen generally prefers the verbal noun to the usual nominative form. In his work death and murder become "dying" and "killing"; heavenly trees have a "white standing"; a supernatural being does not sing or wake, but has "a singing" and "a waking"; humanity's travels become its "going," "walking," or "journeying." I suspect that the somewhat eccentric persistency of this usage follows Patchen's attempts to stress process rather than stasis, to reconcile the meaning of concepts with the energy they represent in the world of becoming. "I separate the seeing," he writes in "The Forms of Knowledge," "from the thing seen." Another favorite locution brings concrete and abstract nouns together in order to lend some sensual reality to otherwise unimaginable concepts—"the shorelights of heaven," the white "columns of death," the "velvet rag of my fear."

"Of the Same Beauty" only hints quietly at another key element of Patchen's middle style. His adaptation and exploitation of the imagistic elements of depth psychology are better illustrated by this passage from "An Examination into Life and Death":

> No one has really fallen
> Whose house was prepared by fire.
> Beneath the Life-Tree
> The still figures rise to the sun,
> And they are enveloped in skins of joy O they fall not
> As we fall who are not yet arrived to taste journeys.

I don't know how much of Carl Jung's work Patchen either ingested or believed, but the language here clearly parallels, at least, the archetypology of Jung's dramatic metaphysics, and a Jungian vocabulary characterizes Patchen's art from *First Will & Testament* through even the last poem-paintings. In this passage, as elsewhere, the conjunction of theological and psychiatric symbology is a visible seam in Patchen's attempt to unite the infinite vistas of inner and external supernature and weave a new language for the vision of transformation.

Although Patchen usually adopts only one of his three modes for any particular poem, he will on occasion parlay the peculiar strengths of his plain and middle style. These mixtures never result in anything quite so electrifying as Whitman's junctures of highfalutin foreign words with American slang ("I loiter enjoying his repartee and his shuffle and breakdown"), and, in fact, Patchen makes no attempt to join modes within a single phrase. He uses them rather to identify separate attitudes within a poem and to let them comment on each other:

> Come back when the fog drifts out over the city
> And sleep puts her kind hands on all these poor devils
>
> Come back when the policeman is in another street
> And Beatrice will let you see her thin soul under the paint
>
> Come back to the corner and tell them what brand of poison
>   you want
> Ask them why your very own dear lady is always on the lay
>   "He Was Alone (as in Reality) upon His Humble Bed"

The gradual shift from the middle to the plain style is repeated inversely at the end of the poem, so that the middle style frames, interprets, and mourns the condition of life described in the defensively tough language of the street.

In "Though I Had Much More to Say" a similar juxtaposition of styles is used to identify a theme that had been hidden beneath an ostensibly careless narrative toughness. The poem is about its speaker's death in war, and, until its conclusion, it is told in Patchen's familiar detective-magazine vocabulary. Its final stanzas are:

> We heard the iron breath of a plane going over
> And I had to look twice at my cards.
> It made its dirt up ahead somewhere.
>
> Have I neglected anything?
> Yes, a shower of stars
> Folded around us
> Falling like white moss from an imperial wall.

The delicate indirection by which death is described not only throws the bravura evocation of warfare into suddenly stark relief, but also recharacterizes the speaker and comments by extension on the values war destroys. Both of these poems typify Patchen's juxtaposition of styles, because they bring more than one valid judgment, each with its attendant emotion, into play.

Ultimately, of course, a poet's choice of language is important as it creates an imagery. Like all romantics, Patchen relies chiefly on metaphor—the imagery meant to transform the perceptual world, rather than to explain it, as simile does. Even when (as often) he uses the form of similitude—"I have seen the crippled lark rise like a dream"—the image changes reality; it does not reinforce our sense of what is real by comparing the unknown to the known. In an organic poetic, responding to an organic universe, an assumption that there is an essential difference between things—the logic by which simile works—would be disruptive. Patchen, predictably, goes to the other extreme. His respect for the integrity of what he calls "the one creature which everything is" sometimes shifts his fundamental metaphor into personification:

> I'd like to die like this . . .
> with the dark fingers of the water
> closing and unclosing over these sleepy lights
> > "Crossing on Staten Island Ferry"

This demand for imaginative synthesis results naturally in attempts to bring together things or qualities that are normally incongruous. In his search after the language of transformation, Patchen's imagery is often elaborate, even conceited, and it sometimes becomes forced, or derivatively surrealistic. When it works, however, it provokes a startled recognition. Falling asleep after sexual intercourse is a movement of being like the darting of a "fish's shadow." Orgasm itself is "a pouring of salt." Seen from a distance, the helmets of Pilate's soldiers are "silver teeth in the sun." These evocative perceptions are intended to renew the reader's sense of the way in which a particular natural experience can lead the awakened consciousness to the experience of mystical unity. Patchen's intuition of nature as a kind of cabalistic language in which one's inspired naming opens a way to the sources of the mystery is, of course, an expression of one of his traditional affinities. His explanation of the process in "Continuation of the Landscape":

> through the mastery and knowledge
> of natural signs we can renew
> ourselves with an ancient innocence

could have been made by either Emerson or Whitman.

The triumph over barriers and achievement of transcendence are invoked also in Patchen's frequent use of synesthesia, as well as in the alchemical Jungian imagery that attempts to reach into some racial memory for symbols of naked being. Jung's system not only brings Patchen metaphors for the definition of individual poems, but also suggests a cosmic drama in which archetypal figures (maiden, horseman, wise old man, soldier, and so forth) act out the eternal processes. In other words, the final extension of metaphor we must consider in discussing Patchen's imagery is metaphor become myth. The transformation implicit in metaphorical comparison is taken literally and put into action. Like all mythologies, Patchen's seeks to explain phenomena by making a fiction, and the terms of the explanation are his own. He does not adapt classic or Hebraic myth, but rather, like Franz Kafka or Hermann Hesse, invents his own more or less coherent cosmology of mythological character and supernatural behavior to explain the doings of the visible world.

The first distinct tendencies toward a personal mythology appear in *First Will & Testament*, where they are, however, subordinate to other concerns. We do not come across true mythological narrative until the appearance in *The Teeth of the Lion* (1942) of "The Reason for Skylarks," a poem which purports to explain the "unpremeditated art" symbolized by the songbird of Shelley's ode. Like much of Patchen's mythological material, this poem about anger and frustration expresses a vision of art as a defiant refusal to admit failure and a protest against cosmic injustice. In a spiritual setting, but one from which our world is visible, fabulous characters represent the invisible causes that affect humanity, and the method, amplified, made even more mysterious by the use of hermetic names, is worked into an extensive analogue of spiritual reality in *The Dark Kingdom*.

The imagery of transformation in this provocative book operates unusually clearly in the poem with the long title "Written After Reading an Item in the Paper about a Young Lady Who Went Mad upon Forsaking Her Lover. He is Here Assumed to Speak." The title is the only explanation of the mythological action, which opens with an idyllic description of the natural love between the speaker and his mistress. Her betrayal of their relationship is presented as a boredom with love, with the "common mysteries" themselves, and her insanity is symbolized by her entrance into the "Anthian Cave" where dwells the apparently divine "Horror" who attacks human love, and in killing it kills also her "self." Although we should be warned that the poems of *The Dark Kingdom* are almost never similarly allegorical, "Written After Reading an Item" is a good example of the way Patchen's mythological apparatus works to find firm metaphorical moorings for our emotion. The physical image of the sinister Anthian cave expresses the almost tactile desperation involved in trying to reach someone caught in the loneliness of insanity.

Because the Horror that disrupts the life in nature of the lovers is a supernatural being, and because the entire action is vaguely felt to possess a ceremonial significance, this mournful poem can also represent the strong theological overtones in *The Dark Kingdom*. The whole book builds purposefully toward a triumphant myth about the beauty and terror of holiness—especially as people search it out of their subconscious shadows. Thus Patchen's use of darkness as moral metaphor. It is not based on the traditional schematization of moral qualities in black and white, but rather on the organic metaphor of darkness as Saint John of the Cross uses it. Analogous to the warm darkness preceding birth, it is the condition of a disciplined consciousness in the final, terrible period before illumination.

Even outside *The Dark Kingdom*, this mythic cosmology is one of the fundamental modes to which Patchen continually returns for his poetry. It provides an imagery by which the emotion of much nonmythological verse is heightened and by which the reality a poem reflects can be extended into normally inaccessible states of being—as in the vision of the silent children who "grovel down the valley of sleep," not remembering "the slow step of the mules/ As they descended the hills lost in the snow," which introduces us to the dream kingdom of "All the Bright Foam of Talk." It is continued also as the informing mode of many of those later poems in which Patchen seeks to demonstrate the truth of Herman Melville's famous suggestion that "the invisible spheres were formed in fright." In "The Great-Sledmakers" (from *The Famous Boating Party*), for instance, Patchen uses the imagery of giantism to describe the activity of colossal craftsmen as during thousands of years they manufacture vehicles big enough to delight the race of giants, but which are, of course, massively destructive in the human world. When a great-sled accidentally slips away, as great-sleds sometimes do (for the Great-Sledmakers drink), it causes natural cataclysms. The tone of this poem is superficially comic, even playful, but it is also frightened. That ambivalent openendedness and its implications might remind us once more of Patchen's refusal to restrict or categorize his realities. Everywhere we find him he is determined (whether successfully or not) to liberate his subject by the radical liberation of his method. He wants an extreme art that is free to go where essences are, either back totally into darkness or all the way out into the light.

Chapter 7

Mysticism and

Social Protest

Further, we take our stand that spiritual evolution is a fact, perhaps the most important fact about us. From this it follows that a community of saints or gnostic beings, sādhúnaṁ rājyam, or a Kingdom of Heaven upon Earth, is a realizable ideal and must one day be realized. The future belongs to the mystics, not as a sect but as an image of man to be.
—Sisirkumar Ghose, *Mystics and Society*

Mysticism has been the ferment of the faiths, the forerunner of spiritual liberty, the inaccessible refuge of the nobler heretics, the inspirer, through poetry, of countless youth who know no metaphysics, the teacher, through the devotional books, of the despairing, the comforter of those who are weary of finitude.
—Josiah Royce, *The World and the Individual*

It was perhaps inevitable that in the secularized, predominantly Protestant culture of the United States one of the most persistent misunderstandings of mysticism would be that it is radically other-worldly or unrealistic. Indeed, although most of Patchen's critics have called him a mystic, they have generally associated that concept with social evasiveness and a tendency to retreat from issues. The usage is loose rather than deliberately reductive, but the common suggestion that Patchen "escapes into mysticism" from the real world he cannot face without terror[1] is nevertheless damaging. An uninitiated reader might almost be led to assume that there were two Kenneth Patchens: one the brash, bitter social poet of "Street Corner College," the other a dreamy contemplator of private kingdoms.

For Patchen, however, as for the mystical writers to whom he is related, the critical function is integrally part of the vision. This attitude has produced a peculiarly American literature of engagement and a typically expansive critical method, neither of which have been sufficiently emphasized in discussions of Whitman and his influence on twentieth-century American utopianism. Thus, brief attention to the kinship between *Democratic Vistas* and such books as Van Wyck Brooks's *America's Coming-of-Age*, Waldo Frank's *The Re-Discovery of America*, William Carlos Williams's *In the American Grain*, John Steinbeck's *Log* from *Sea of Cortez*, Lewis Mumford's *The Conduct of Life*, and Henry Miller's *The Air-Conditioned Nightmare* may prove useful here. Although these social studies may vary widely in certain fundamental attitudes—from the insistent teleology of Mumford and Whitman, for instance, to the equally insistent nonteleology of Steinbeck or the determined indifference to such matters of Williams—they share assumptions about the definition of community, the relation of the individual to it, the value of the primitive, and the uses of indirection that identify a common allegiance. Their variations on these and other Whitmanian themes can be worked into a preliminary examination of their subgenre and applied to our immediate purpose of approaching Patchen. After 1936 he was not in the habit of articulating his premises, and by clarifying the general background of his protest writing we may be able to account for his characteristic tone and manner. To such pragmatic considerations we may add that several of these studies are excellent in themselves.

Whitmanian social analysts base their systems upon some personal intuition of organic unity, but, for each of them, cosmic wisdom, when it is truly wise, is returned to the earth and human affairs. Although they rarely speak to specific issues, they are critics and reformers. "I beat the gong of revolt," Whitman once wrote. He meant it. Especially in light of Whitman's popular reputation as the complacent champion of American boosterism, it is noteworthy that Ralph Chaplin, the propagandist for the Industrial Workers of the World who had little patience for anything but his cause, found that the old poet brought him to metaphysics despite himself. In his autobiography, Chaplin wrote that Whitman's work had been recommended "as rebel poetry of the highest order. One Sunday I opened *Leaves of Grass* at random. It was a revelation. From that moment on Karl Marx and Kropotkin had very keen competition."[2] A similar significance might be discovered in the lifelong reverence for Whitman and his work that Eugene Debs expressed in his famous pilgrimage to Camden.[3]

The basis for the revolutionary impulse that Chaplin, Debs, and others admired in Whitman is simply that the experienced knowledge of unity creates an awareness of both human stature and proper relationships to which the existing society must be compared. Rather than adopt economic or political criteria, Whitman and his successors criticize according to the degree to which their society conforms to some universal order. That is, they analyze society according to demands it would not recognize and goals it would not understand. One definitive example of this critical method (which is, of course, utilized by many religious systems) is offered by *Democratic Vistas*, the most influential of American mystical social documents, and the work to which Whitman's supporters point to demonstrate his awareness of the social and moral problems in American life. With its lofty overview of history and culture and its insistence on the spiritual significance of democracy, *Democratic Vistas* develops an absolute standard for the conduct of American civilization. Whitman allows no compromise: either American democracy is to be the culmination of history and the great spiritual achievement of the human race or it will degenerate into a condition "equivalent, in its real world, to that of the fabled damned."

In view of Whitman's use of such exalted criteria, it makes little sense to remark, as Richard Chase did in *Walt Whitman Reconsidered*, that *Democratic Vistas'* social theory is amateurish or naive.[4] Whitman is so indifferent to political demands in his essay that it seems perverse to use them in judging him. He speaks from the point of view of one who has recognized the principle of wholeness. His fundamental criterion for the spiritual quality of American life is whether the individual can be whole in it, whether the structure of democracy, which is not of the least importance in itself, defends and encourages the wholeness of individual citizens. Outside of a few revolutionary suggestions for the reform of democratic institutions, the chief means by which he would reconstruct society is personalism, which, although it might solve political problems, is itself hardly accessible to political establishment.

Whitman influenced later writers by his messianic promise to America, prophetic denunciation of its failures, and the definitions of democracy and democratic virtue that attended his vision of a new world triumphant. With these ideas as a working basis, his successors sought to develop a social ethic which would advance the special American destiny. The first of the important Whitmanian social philosophies appeared in the young Van Wyck Brooks's *America's Coming-of-Age*, published in 1915, twenty-three years after the master's death. In this influential study, Brooks diagnosed the problem in American life according to the split of cultural types into "highbrow" and "lowbrow." His highbrow was, in essence, the intellectual, his lowbrow the common man, and there was no interaction between them. Both were self-contained, defensive, and incapable of effective action. Not only did this disastrous split impede progress, it stifled the growth of the person, and for Brooks as for Whitman "the only serious approach to society is the personal approach."[5]

Brooks's answer, or, rather, the hero he invoked in a situation he described with some apprehension, was Walt Whitman himself, who combined both highbrow and lowbrow in his person and thus could act effectively in his culture. For his exemplary Whitman, Brooks went not to the poetry but to the poet's moving descriptions of his activity among the wounded in an army hospital, arguing that Whitman's ability to communicate with the soldiers on a cultural level different from that typically expected of an important intellectual bridged the difference between cultural types. The importance of Brooks's emphasis on Whitman the person rather than Whitman the literatus was perhaps recognized by Waldo Frank when, in a review of American cultural criticism he appended to *The Re-Discovery of America*, he praised Brooks for interpreting American culture in terms of "energy" rather than "forms." Brooks, like Frank and others after him, felt his task was not so much to interpret the meaning of what Whitman said as it was to tap the spiritual or psychological force that Whitman discovered at the sources of democracy.[6]

Frank, an early friend and associate of Brooks, continued in his own prolific career a missionary Whitmanian criticism, probably most importantly in *The Re-Discovery of America* (1929). This ambitious study intellectualizes and schematizes the method of Whitman and most of his successors, and thus is exemplary in assumption and logic, if not always in quality. Frank applies apparently distant mystical attitudes to specific social conditions and establishes a system of explanation and judgment by which visionary truth is put to work in the familiar world. His basic concept and standard is the idea of universal "Wholeness," the state to which all people and, in effect, all cultures aspire. Persons who know the whole in the same experiential way that they know their own bodies, "without abandoning the personal," are mystics. Their sense of the whole is the "mystic sense."[7] Cultures possess wholeness to the extent that they relate the natural and supernatural worlds and thus discover an order by which individuals can live in harmony with the processes of being. Medieval Christian Europe, Frank suggests, was an example. People lived in it "as cells within a body."

Because it cannot now be expressed in meaningful action and because Christendom mistook its institutions (church, state, ego) for metaphysical entities, the wholeness of the European past is no longer valid. The church, nation-state, and other vestiges of the European experiment are now merely the agents of an empty ritual. When Americans rely on their sterile forms, they bind themselves to the corpse of Europe. In Frank's analysis, the most telling measure of our failure as a nation is that we have not built a culture according to the potential native wholeness that was discovered and incarnated by Walt Whitman.

Frank argues further that the person (or the culture) who is denied the experience of wholeness will mistake a part for the whole and behave as if that little fragment exhausted reality. Such error undermines modern culture and leads to "atomization"— fragmentation of vision so thorough that in its extreme state (contemporary American civilization) the individual ego is considered not only real but the final justification for action. The localizing of authority and meaning, which characterizes American groups as well as individuals, creates a culture oriented to power rather than love. Frank defines these terms as antithesis: love is "the principle of union, of order, of creation" (189); power is action for the benefit of the personal ego, "the principle of chaos" (189).

Out of this loose dialectic Frank analyzes, sometimes acutely, the faults of his culture. He is able to explain the day-to-day operations of even such minor institutions as baseball and can discuss newswriting with as much sympathetic intellectual power as he brings to Goethe. His idea of a lost wholeness provides a vocabulary for discussions of political and artistic failures. The American Constitution, for instance, is an artificial wholeness created out of an unnatural combination of political and religious systems in order to defend a conservative ideal which is essentially British in origin. Similarly, American artists, Frank feels, are loyal to the fragmented wholeness of a moribund Europe, and their art reflects or apologizes for power. Using this hypothesis, he can pair such apparently disparate figures as T. S. Eliot and Irving Berlin as nostalgic romantics who derive their theory from the detritus of European tradition, and between whom there is, aesthetically, little to choose.

Frank's analysis of what is wrong with our culture may be often sententious and reductive, but it is consistent, morally earnest, and at least usually true. His recommendations for positive action are less convincing, even though his basic principle seems sound: he argues that our society is chaotic and that, instead of resisting chaos, we must acknowledge and embrace it in order to wring an organic wholeness from it. The specifics of the embrace, however, are left vague. In describing the function of his exemplary "Groups" in the building of a whole America, Frank falls back on evasive cliches: the groups will act "according to the American Dream" or to implement the national destiny. When he turns to his neo-Oriental "technic" for expanding awareness, an exercise which supposedly leads to the personal experience of wholeness, the entire project comes to smack of the fashionable cultisms he usually has the good taste to avoid.

In the broadest terms, the failures of *The Re-Discovery of America* are due to Frank's apparent inability to feel what he is

saying. Despite that, his mystical standard and his basic struc-
ture—a statement of cosmology followed by a cosmological analy-
sis of a wide range of American subjects—are those of many
better books. William Carlos Williams's *In The American Grain*
(1925), for instance, had already utilized much the same method
as Frank, although more subtly and with greater feeling for the life
of the subject. While praising *In The American Grain* in his
appendix to *Re-Discovery*, Frank complained that Williams had
not done enough "to define the values by which he paints his
portraits," but Frank wasn't looking closely. Williams shapes and
judges his characters according to their conformity to the entire
meaning and possibility of American life—a standard closely re-
lated to Frank's idea of wholeness. He says as much in his little
preface, in which he describes his attempt to "re-name" American
experience, and concludes: "it has been my wish to draw from
every source one thing, the strange phosphorus of the life, name-
less under an old misappelation."[8]

Williams's purpose is to expose and attack the failures of
American society, but his analysis is typically Whitmanian in its
removal from muckraking. Although he occasionally breaks into
invective against immediate abuses, he is concerned with getting
at sources, with defining both the nature of America and the
fundamental failure of its culture. He criticizes contemporary con-
ditions (as in the opening of "Jacataqua") only as an example of
the principle of decadence working in history. For Williams,
America is or should be a spiritual agency, and his vision of it is
surprisingly like that of his nineteenth-century precursors: it is a
free Edenic world where people are able to rid themselves of the
past and its decadence by accepting newness and freedom for what
they are.

America fails, however, because Americans lack the courage
to live in Eden. European migrants, lonely without the trappings
of their old home, imposed familiar patterns on unfamiliar phe-
nomena. They named things according to traditional categories
and so obscured both their newness and their value. Williams
holds the Puritans of New England most responsible for the estab-
lishment of an alien culture, but the pattern by which the failures
of the old world are repeated in the new are as old as American

history itself. Even in the pre-Columbian opening sketch, "Red Eric," the quarrels of Europe are carried to the shores of Vinland and the primordial fratricide reenacted. Williams's subsequent essays become variations on the theme of American failure, and his book is, in one sense, an anatomy of the historical inability of Americans to live the American life. He finds that inability so deeply imbedded in our history and our culture that he finally accepts explicitly the same pattern of destruction and rebuilding that we noticed earlier in his literary theory, as well as in those of Patchen and Miller: "We must go back to the beginning; it must all be done over; everything that is must be destroyed" (215).

In the American Grain was one culmination of a widespread but loosely defined interest in Whitmanian cultural analysis and historiography that developed during the years around World War I and flourished in the decade following. It also informs such exemplary texts as Hart Crane's *The Bridge*, Jean Toomer's *Cane*, John Dos Passos's *The 42nd Parallel*, and many of Lewis Mumford's early books. These writers were angrily critical about American culture, but (with the possible exception of Dos Passos) they also clung to a fundamentally optimistic vision of some spiritual or ethical utopia, and their collective voice, although never silenced, was all but overwhelmed by the many aggressively materialistic and partisan voices of the Great Depression. Perhaps it was only coincidence that a new group of important neo-Whitmanian social documents appeared during the years of and just after World War II and seemed to respond indirectly to it. Henry Miller's *The Air-Conditioned Nightmare* (1945) renews many of the terms and attitudes of the personally focused cultural analyses of the twenties. John Steinbeck's *Log* from *Sea of Cortez* (1941) adapts the common method to scientific inquiry. Lewis Mumford's *The Conduct of Life* (1951) coordinates and extends most of the powers Whitmanian analysis developed over the years.

The Air-Conditioned Nightmare is Miller's account of his own rediscovery of America after he was forced to leave Europe at the onset of the war. Like *Democratic Vistas* or *In the American Grain*, it attempts to invent an America or to discover the new myth out of which a nation may grow. The study Miller calls "The Air-Conditioned Nightmare" is actually contained loosely in two volumes, and projects a third volume about the transcendental America that could be. Like many of Miller's plans, this one was conceived in enthusiasm rather than reflection and was eventually abandoned. *The Air-Conditioned Nightmare* is a thematically unified book, but *Remember to Remember* (1947), which is subtitled "Vol. 2 of the Air-Conditioned Nightmare," is more a collection of miscellaneous essays. It includes, however, two of Miller's funniest contributions to the analysis of America—"The Staff of Life," on American bread, and "Astrological Fricassee," on Hollywood—as well as "The Most Lovely Inanimate Object in Existence," a prose-poem about the mystical qualities of the land that an uninformed but sensitive observer might guess belonged among the lyrical passages of *In the American Grain*. The study, then, runs naturally from the preface of *The Air-Conditioned Nightmare* to "The Most Lovely Inanimate Object in Existence," which concludes both *Remember to Remember* and the entire thematic sequence. Whatever literary unity the books may possess derives from the consciousness of their author, which is the only principle of unity or consistency in which Miller has ever shown any interest.

In his preface Miller establishes a familiar cosmology as the basis and norm for his study. His universe is substantially that of Emerson, Whitman, and other nineteenth-century romantic writers: humanity is a wholeness in itself and part of a cosmic process of growth. One's true responsibility is to join the universal organism, to rid oneself of personal weakness in order not to resist the impulsion of creative evolution, which is the law controlling the species, if not always the individual. After establishing that context, Miller repeats the familiar accusation that the new world has indeed failed to be new and thus sunk to a moral level inferior to that of even so-called primitive or decadent nations.

The narrative of *The Air-Conditioned Nightmare* opens in Pittsburgh, "in the very quick of the nightmare, in the crucible where all values are reduced to slag."[9] Here, Miller tells us, he has just finished reading about the Indian saint Ramakrishna, a figure to whom he returns throughout the study as a representative of love and wisdom. This contrast of value systems is immediately reinforced by an exhortation to destruction—specifically of those

American values that have created Pittsburgh. When he is in the mood to make judgments, Miller finds scarcely anything American likeable. In *Remember to Remember*, in fact, he defines "American" as "the more set, crass, conservative, prejudiced, stupid, narrow-minded, unexperimental, and unrevolutionary."[10]

Whenever he comes across something that delights him, however, such as the wisdom of the American Indian or the lore of the automobile, Miller forgets to be critical. In much of his narrative he identifies the American failure almost solely by implicit contrast to the series of remarkable characters he encounters along his way. He seems constitutionally incapable of writing anything that does not eventually become a book of marvels, and he has a keen eye for the marvelous in even apparently nondescript individuals—so much so that he is likely in the flush of enthusiasm to mistake the eccentricity for the man. His characteristically motley community of saints includes an automobile mechanic in Albuquerque, a desert rat near the Grand Canyon, a pair of young surrealists in the Middle West, and an ex-convict on a train, as well as more famous people: Abe Rattner, Edgar Varese, Beniamino Bufano. Alfred Stieglitz and John Marin appear in an enthusiastic heroical essay and are of particular interest in linking Miller to several other twentieth-century mystical writers. The great photographer was also a hero to Williams, Frank, and Hart Crane.

As one example of the romantic values he seeks in American life, Miller recounts his visit to "The Shadows," the classic Louisiana home of Weeks Hall. He admires Hall's estate because it has grown naturally out of its own past, culture, and soil. With his enthusiasm for horticulture and his feeling for the balance of living things, Hall has created an exotic garden in which even human constructs share a common life. The vegetation itself re-creates the landscapes of other countries and times, and is one expression of Hall's metaphysics. Miller quotes the gardener and compulsive conversationalist—who is also a prolific painter—as he dreams aloud of designing a garden that is ultimately a transcendental sculpture. By devoting his mystical profundities to the place that gives them form and substance, and thus in a sense making his life into a work of art, Hall has succeeded to a limited degree, Miller thinks, in fulfilling one of the goals of the mystical life.

The special climate Hall and his estate have created is more important than anything they may be in themselves. In it Miller can discover his own transcendences and continue the growth of his own consciousness. Late one night, stimulated by one of his host's cryptic remarks, he is drawn out of the house. Impelled by the presence of the garden, the past, and the moonlight, he kisses the stone lips of the strange goddesses that stand at the corners of the garden, then strolls "back to the trellised garden house which lies on the banks of the Bayou Teche. The scene before my eyes was that of a Chinese painting. Sky and water had become one; the whole world was floating in a nebular mist. It was indescribably beautiful and bewitching. I could scarcely believe that I was in America. . . . I went back to bed and lay there not just wide awake but super-conscious, alive in every tip and pore of my being" (105). This is no beatific vision, and, in fact, Miller makes no special claim for it; but it is an experience of the essential unity of things. Although Miller contrasts it only perfunctorily to the crassness of the materialistic culture around him, or to the parrot-like lives of the tourists who crowd through the Hall estate, it is one clear example of the principle by which he and his host are distinguished from the American mob and its culture, and it identifies one of the fundamental human activities that America has stifled. Such apparently incidental methods of social criticism remain typical of "The Air-Conditioned Nightmare" sequence, even though some of the comic pieces in *Remember to Remember* are, because of their comedy, able to become openly abusive about the perversions Americans have worked upon nature.

Critical indirection is more insistently sustained in John Steinbeck's narrative portion (or *Log*) from *Sea of Cortez*, the ecological study of the littoral in the Gulf of California he produced in collaboration with Ed Ricketts.[11] Here social observations are made almost exclusively by juxtaposing ecological facts with historical and cultural facts according to the rules of an intellectual exercise Steinbeck and Ricketts called "speculative metaphysics." Their object was to enjoy the freedom and creativity of thought without the restrictions of formal validity or demonstration. They emphasized the process rather than the result of thinking and aspired to insight and recognition rather than scientifically verifiable truth. Inevitably, the sympathetic reader must be himself engaged in their stimulating metaphysical game, and, in the various religious, philosophical, scientific, and historical contexts developed by the narrative, wonder if, for instance, a colony of pelagic tunicates (165) does not offer some provocative analogue of the nature and function of human community.

Speculative metaphysics is admittedly a tricky business and its validity for both characters and readers rests on the radical monism which Steinbeck several times defines and to which he tacitly refers questions of significance and judgment. His universe in *Sea of Cortez* is remarkably Emersonian or Taoist, about as purely traditional an expression of nature mysticism as one is likely to find in the twentieth century. Late in the book he describes it in terms of his scientific inquiry:

> Our own interest lay in relationships of animal to animal. If one observes in this relational sense, it seems apparent that species are only commas in a sentence, that each species is at once the point and the base of a pyramid, that all life is relational to the point where an Einsteinian relativity seems to emerge. And then not only the meaning but the feeling about species grows misty. One merges into another, groups melt into ecological groups until the time when what we know as life meets and enters what we think of as non-life: barnacle and rock, rock and earth, earth and tree, tree and rain and air. And the units nestle into the whole and are inseparable from it. Then one can come back to the microscope and the tide pool and the aquarium. But the little animals are found to be changed, no longer set apart and alone. And it is a strange thing that most of the feeling we call religious, most of the mystical outcrying which is one of the most prized and used and desired reactions of our species, is really the understanding and the attempt to say that man is related to the whole thing, related inextricably to all reality, known and unknowable. . . . that all things are one thing and that one thing is all things—plankton, a shimmering

phosphorescence on the sea and the spinning planets and an expanding universe, all bound together by the elastic string of time. (216–17)

That sense of kinship inspires new feelings of loyalty and responsibility. In the implicit but unmistakable network of reference it establishes, Steinbeck is able to make judgments about such matters as character, the uses and abuses of money, points of comparative culture, even the appropriateness of place names, without feeling obliged to interrupt his narrative to argue his point. In one sense, *Sea of Cortez* is the record of a voyage into primitive knowledge and experience, the mysteries of bloodstream and tide pool, where the civilized devices of measurement, category, and scientific prediction, particularly as symbolized by official navigational charts and tables, will not always see the voyager through danger. Here one must supplement the lifeless formal information of the *Coast Pilot* by learning a new motivation and a new standard, which is organic: "the first rule of life is living" (29). Broadly speaking, the desirable or appropriate in *Sea of Cortez* (one hesitates to use moral categories) is that which furthers the survival and growth of the human species, itself integrally part of the grand ecology whose "synonym . . . is ALL" (85).

This rigorous organicism has to do with literary composition as well as meaning, and by respecting its demands Steinbeck can reverse, for instance, the familiar moralism that prohibited sexual frankness in books. He comments on the "bawdiness this book must have if it is to be true" to the impulsions and strategies of life (68). Or he can launch an attack on the corruptions and rapacities of industrial capitalism simply by describing the ecologically destructive operations of a fleet of Japanese shrimpers (3, 247–50). Or, he can consider the war that was just breaking out in Europe. It is only mentioned incidentally, but its implications are developed by analogy in discussions of the belligerency of crayfish (17) or in speculations about the characteristics of dying species (86–88). Steinbeck, of course, first became prominent as a radical social critic and reformer, and, while it would be distortive to look in *Sea of Cortez* for the ideology or methods of *In Dubious Battle*, we should recognize the essentially utopian and prophetic qualities of what remained one of his favorites among his own books.[12]

Lewis Mumford's *The Conduct of Life* is more self-conscious than Steinbeck's book was about claiming the tradition of prophetic, speculative social analysis that derives from the nineteenth-century American romantics. By his title, Mumford invites comparison to Emerson, and in an annotation he characterizes his study as a conscious expansion of the personalism of *Democratic Vistas*.[13] In addition, he was a lifelong friend and ally of Van Wyck Brooks and Waldo Frank, and he acknowledges Frank's concept of the chaotic as a starting point for his own study (15). Like all of the mystical thinkers described here, he bases his system on a "doctrine of the whole" (223–26) and proceeds according to "an organic syncretism" (232–35). Like them also, he alternates complementary negative and positive commentary, develops important historical and scientific evidence, and, despite an insistent universalism, ultimately turns his attention to the enhancement of day-to-day life in the immediate world. He would not always agree with these other writers—in fact, he makes a disparaging allusion to Miller (18)—but his essential kinship to them and his ability to orchestrate many of their isolated ideas and insights make *The Conduct of Life* one major point of culmination and departure on the rising spiral of Whitman's visionary tradition.

The Conduct of Life is a complex, ambitious book, itself a synthesis of many disciplines and philosophies. It aims at nothing less than an extended definition and history of human nature. For our purposes of sketching the outlines of an American genre and illuminating the critical assumptions of an American writer, however, we can limit our consideration to two complementary aspects of it: its working concept of evolution and its contribution to the native theory of personalism. Particularly in his reversal of some uncritical assumptions about evolution, Mumford addresses more persuasively than many of his colleagues difficult questions about the origin and stability of values. The intuitively perceived "whole" to which Frank, Miller, and Steinbeck appeal for moral authority, like the idealized America of Williams, seems sufficiently real and useful in terms of these writers' ability to establish an analytic tool, but the concept necessarily remains frustratingly evasive to the reader, who is obliged either to approximate the mystical or intuitive experience that informs each "wholeness" or to guess at its nature by observing its results.

The holistic standard by which Mumford assesses political, cultural, economic, and personal phenomena avoids some of the embarrassments of ineffability by being accessible to familiar intellectual categories. It also avoids the temptation to impose an essentially static definition (such as "Eden" or even "The Whole") on a reality characterized by incessant, exuberant change. It exists only in the future, and anticipates the realization of every potential attribute and power toward which humanity is evolving. God, Mumford argues, amending the deterministic, mechanical character of many ideas about evolutionary progress, does not originate evolution but lies waiting at the end of it: "The universe does not issue out of God, in conformity with his fiat: it is rather God who in the long processes of time emerges from the universe, as the far-off event of creation and the ultimate realization of the person toward which creation seems to move" (71). It follows then that "man's business becomes not so much the mere contemplation as the active creation of the divine" (72). This theory about the ends of evolution and the authority of the future has probably been partially recognized and unwittingly applied by a number of mystical writers who could not have articulated it so clearly.[14]

Because the divine goal of creative evolution is personal, the evolutionary agency must be human. In Mumford's scheme as in Whitman's, personality is an advanced condition, which is not originally part of human nature, but is attained through a process of evolution that cannot operate independently of human cooperation. Once the species has developed beyond significant biological change, evolution becomes essentially psychic, a function of an increasingly complex, mutually inspiring interrelationship of individual and society. In crude outline, the process is this: primitive man has only a partial hold on his humanity; his identity is tribal, his powers of introspection minimal, his physical, intellectual, and spiritual life characterized by repetition and limitation. Outside of the sacredness assigned by birth to a few special individuals (king, priest), his society offers no variety of roles through which the individual may distinguish his particular quality and importance. The transformation of primitive man and the emergence of the person is the result of a mysterious event which Mumford identifies chiefly according to the conditions accompanying it: the development by society of a sufficient range of possible occupational and domestic roles that individuals can imagine a different self, and the influence of an extended "Time of Troubles," when the traditional rewards of tribal society seem no longer attainable or worthwhile.

Under such circumstances the exceptional individual may withdraw from tribal life, reject its limitations, and, becoming a person, transcend its categories. At least imaginatively, he transforms himself into a citizen of the world and introduces to it previously undreamed of possibilities of freedom and redemption. Thus, as Mumford argues in Emersonian terms, "the birth of a universal personality is the equivalent, if not more than the equivalent, of the sudden appearance of a new species in nature" (98). His primary examples are Jesus, Confucius, Buddha, and other founders of universalist religions and philosophies. As they establish social roles and personal models by which others may discover possibilities for personal identity, the lives and teachings of such persons radically transform society. "The rites of sex and marriage," Mumford writes, "the conduct of economic life and the administration of government, in the end every social institution must be altered so as to support the new person and make possible his social existence and his participation in all the activities from which, in the first instance, he had withdrawn and had apparently left behind him" (102–3). This reorganization encourages new transformations of tribal individuals, whose own revolutionary attainments of personality transform society once again. The unending process whereby the person and society continually inform and stimulate the growth of each other can presumably be limited only by stifling the daring and creativity of the human species. At the end of it all waits a possibility of God.

The demands of the moral life inherent in such a cosmology, the relationship of the person to history and community, and his responsibility to both, are rigorous and unmistakable. In fact, the need to conform one's behavior to the purposes of the awakening god of the future establishes a categorical imperative. By the simple acts of being human and recognizing the implications of humanity, one is engaged in a difficult but ennobling struggle for freedom, creativity, and, ultimately, transcendence. Each moment is charged with moral attention and energy, and the personal stakes are high. Failure or indifference can never be inconsequential. Individuals (or nations) who do not serve the universal human community of the present and, through it, the divine community to come may be counted among the fabled damned indeed.

Mumford's exhaustiveness and precision of context permit him to make innumerable judgments on every aspect of human activity, from diet and clothing to the nature of good and evil themselves. He exploits that capacity most fully in the detailed curriculum for the integration and renewal of life with which he concludes his study, and which justifies his title. With his ability to move from the olympian perspective to the minute particular, Mumford earns an unusual degree of prophetic stature. He seems free to speak out without rehearsal or self-consciousness, whether in magnanimity or wrath, about the times and the manners of the various communities, local or global, he addresses. His book is a kind of refreshing bath for intellect and spirit; it returns the receptive reader to the very origins and nature of the moral life.

Kenneth Patchen differs from other American mystical social critics in several ways. With the exception of the early Steinbeck, he is alone in being best known, even typed, as a protest writer of a particularly uncompromising and vitriolic kind. He is also disinclined to explain or apply himself in book-length studies; his analyses are characteristically limited to the length of a poem or a few sentences of prose. More consequentially, he stands apart on a basic philosophical premise. His ideas about humanity and the universe are generally consistent with the Whitmanian synthesis, except that he (with William Carlos Williams) apparently does not acknowledge the possibilities of social or psychic evolution on which Whitman, Frank, Miller, and Mumford base their critical systems and, ultimately, their optimism. That he rejects, as it were, the consolations of evolutionary destiny leaves him at something of a loss to reconcile his exaltation of innocence with his horrified recognition of the atrocities men and women have historically perpetrated against each other. He is thus more easily hurt than the others, angrier, more inclined to bitterness. Such an orientation and vulnerability has its costs, of course, but it also encourages, or even forces, Patchen to a fierce concentration on the social conditions and institutions that are poisoning the present.

Although such differences particularize Patchen, the force and accuracy of his analysis is in many ways more immediately a function of his kinship with other Whitmanian philosophers and artists. Like them, he has always maintained aggressively that social statement is inseparable from mystical vision. In his introduction to *Job*, he described his beloved William Blake as "perhaps the greatest social realist of his age—the bitter immediacy of his symbolism is as much grounded in the Industrial Revolution in England as it is in his own special 'Country' (of the naked and majestic Soul)." The remark might be equally relevant to Patchen's own work, which finds its origins in the language and issues of the Great Depression as much as in the cabalistic landscapes of the Dark Kingdom. Even before he abandoned the more or less Marxist stance of *Before the Brave*, however, the standards by which Patchen criticized both American and world affairs were essentially those of Whitman and the other writers already discussed: society is evil as it interferes with the natural, which is defined by innocence, organicism, and spontaneous love. The critic who passes judgment on such things speaks from the vantage point of the whole and defines problems according to their deviations from the laws governing the entire cosmic organism, rather than by analyzing economic law, political structure, or any other purely social system. Moral responsibility, he understands, is not legalistic, but is immediately dependent upon enlightened perception. Finally, Patchen shares with many of his colleagues a conviction that such knowledge is subversive and that the greatest poets and seers are the chief enemies of the state.

The idea that the artist is necessarily both rebel and outcast is at least as old as Taoism in Asia and Plato in the West. As a law of Patchen's world, it offers one access to the entire body of his protest writing. Waldo Frank concluded his early *Our America*

(1919) with the contention that "in a dying world, creation is revolution," and Patchen's work corroborates the insight. *Before the Brave* has as one of its basic themes that creativity is the ultimate political crime. The argument is made, and a lifelong pessimism about the possibility of social reform introduced, in "Joe Hill Listens to the Praying," which is set in the prison yard in Salt Lake City moments before the legendary Wobbly songwriter is executed for murder. As the prison chaplain reads an inanely irrelevant petition for divine pardon, Joe Hill faces the rifles of the firing squad, and an unidentified narrator (probably as the collective voice of the I.W.W.) celebrates both the individual career and the Wobbly movement in a free verse interspersed with fragments of Hill's revolutionary songs.

After he has established the physical situation of the poem, the narrator moves quickly into Wobbly lore with his celebration of the migratory bindlestiff culture which drew strength from the American myth of the hobo as the free soul in nature. Then he contrasts the natural life in an eroticized landscape with the repressiveness of American society. The inherent contradictions between freedom and social structures give way—as an implied answer—to a lyrical catalogue of the great events in Wobbly history. As the narrator becomes increasingly involved in memories of the movement, the emotion of his poem builds almost to rapture in an evocation of Wobbly singing and a chanting of the slogan, "One Big Union."

Just as we and the narrator are about to become completely caught up in revolutionary ardor, however, a scrap of the chaplain's prayer breaks the rising emotion and returns us to the scene in the courtyard, where the image of Joe Hill and the rifles reminds us that a revolution and its hope have failed. The tone falters momentarily as the narrator accepts defeat, and in the only rhymed lines of his own making echoes ironically the famous refrain from Hill's "The Preacher and the Slave":

> There are no soap boxes in the sky.
> We won't eat pie, now, or ever
> when we die

But if a communal movement is crushed a communal art remains.

The songs, "that now are part of more than any of us," "had hair and blood on them" and their influence ends the poem on a note that is at once helpless, defiant, and triumphant. Its feeling for art as a redemptive activity in despite of essentially hopeless social conditions informs all of Patchen's work from this point forward:

> Let them burn us, hang us, shoot us,
>
> Joe Hill,
>
> For at the last we had what it takes
> to make songs with.

Beyond the quality of the poem and its thematic significance at the outset of Patchen's career, the choice of Joe Hill and the Industrial Workers of the World as the central figures in a fierce American social drama is provocative. The mysterious but attractive songwriter and martyr, at once a tough migrant worker and an intellectual hero who concluded his repudiation of murder charges with the defiant, "I have lived like an artist and I shall die like an artist,"[15] becomes representative of the entire romantic mythology of the I.W.W. and its anarchistic revolution. The Wobblies (at least those who wrote for the *Songbook* and the *Industrial Worker*, and adopted the colorful nicknames of the lumber camps) were themselves Whitmanian critics of society, who practiced a crude form of the open road philosophy and thought of themselves as pioneers of the democratic life. In fact, the imbalance in the primitive personalism they developed unawares provides one clue to their eventual failure as a union. Wobblies were, finally, more concerned with their own exercise of freedom than with the exigencies of the labor movement. Their spontaneous community of fellow workers was too idealistically conceived, and their organization inevitably collapsed into its own individualisms. The conflict between freedom and organization is particularly troubling to all anarchists. Patchen himself, who, as Kenneth Rexroth notes, shares the loyalties of the old revolution of the world,[16] seems reluctantly to have come to the conclusion that any organization for social change defeats its own purpose, because organizations are inherently corrupt.

In keeping with his distrust of what Waldo Frank called "Power Groups," Patchen did not persist in the political contentiousness of

Before the Brave. In fact, he abandoned all revolutionary weapons except creativity. Because he understands and can to some extent guide the forces shaping human affairs, the idealized poet of Patchen's subsequent work represents the natural order, which is the great danger to artificial orders built on crime and fear. In *The Re-Discovery of America*, Frank insisted that creativity is a function of love and that love is subversive in a world which relies on power. That paraphrase is especially pertinent to Patchen, whose whole notion of poetry was bound up in his defense of love against the modern world. His fixation on love resulted naturally from his emotional makeup and reflects the necessity that the poet return to basic personal things if he is to find principles that will not betray themselves. Such a social program is ultimately neither social nor programmatic; it rests in the Emersonian and Whitmanian idea that the poet is an agent of cosmic order, who contributes to the growth of the wholeness to which all humanity belongs by cultivating self-knowledge and, after that, spiritual self-reliance. Patchen's statement in "The Village Tudda"—"I believe that to deliver myself/ Is to deliver you"[17]—echoes one of the most familiar Whitmanian notions of poetic responsibility and power.

Beyond that, Patchen had no orthodoxy to promote. In fact, he resisted gathering anything more than the rudiments of a coherent body of fixed belief by which incidents could be judged. Although soon past Marxism, he continued to believe that economic oppression was the basic evil in American society, and he was contemptuous of capitalism and its ethics. Organized religion he considered obscene. In the *Journal* Albion Moonlight is made to call Christ, Joseph, and Mary "images in a vicious tale that gluts on the animal blood of our race." Politically, Patchen was a philosophical anarchist and a radical pacifist who believed uncompromisingly that any institution by which human life is taken is fiendish:

> This
> is a man. You are not to kill him.
>
> This is a man. He has a poor time in the world.
> You are not to kill him.

This is a man. There is a purpose in his being here.
You are not to kill him.

"The Battle of Unameit"

The prohibition of murder in all its forms, spiritual and physical, is perhaps Patchen's only negative commandment, and he feels it is the social duty of the poet, the public conscience, to repeat the injunction unceasingly to a world that is remarkably adept at forgetting it. He outlines both his responsibility and his frustration in "Can the Harp Shoot Through Its Propellers?" Although the morality fashioned in love ("*the secret of your earth*") is wasted on a people scampering frantically after illusory goals ("a blind man, passing/ In great haste, bumped my arm and gave/ My words upon the dusty wind"), the poet must not abandon his moral position. He must continue to resist the blandishments of the "damn beasts" who wish to enlist him in their causes, not understanding "that the fashion of my art/ Could not design a submarine or bomb a city."

Because he himself best embodies his morality, Patchen often protests by placing himself or a surrogate in a sensitive situation and reporting it according to its emotional impact upon him. He only rarely analyzes or explains. His basic point of view and the techniques by which he implements it can be illustrated by several poems from *First Will & Testament*, one of his most successful books of protest writing and the one which set the style and pace of later work. His techniques, of course, attempt simultaneously to describe the moral event, envision the universal nature which is its context, and record the judgment of it. Thus description often becomes grotesque or hallucinatory. In "Behold, One of Several Little Christs," for example, modern warfare is defined by an almost consistently medieval symbolism. Punctuated by a series of italicized Whitmanian "I am's," which establish the authority of the poet, the narrative describes the crucifixion of an innocent girl by the modern "Leader," Leather Face, and the action is occasionally as frenzied as a Flemish interpretation of death:

Not believing the stuff about flags after you have seen a man
dance

Rope-necked on a dirty platform and the pretty girls yelling
   like mad
Moving their thighs as though Death were coming into them
   too.

The significance of the torture and its effect on everyone who
collaborates or out of apathy permits it to happen (nearly all
civilized persons) is then in part defined by the use of animal
grotesques ("There is the sneer of the bat and the gull's fang,/
There is a lobster beating his breast and singing"). The poem
reaches its climax in a geographical image that exaggerates the
physical quality of death until it corresponds to its symbolic di-
mension:

We looked again at the maps and a little stream of her blood
Had made a river that we had no fit equipment to cross
And her hand had fallen over the city that we hoped to take

The dramatization by which the poet participates in the action of
"Behold, One of Several Little Christs," is also used to good
effect in the strange narrative about capitalism and its wars that
builds to a shocking conclusion in "Man Is to Man a Beast." The
poem opens in a battle scene which parodies the cliches of war
fiction, as the narrator leads an attack on a town for the purpose of
rescuing a mysterious "her." His record of the fighting is dis-
jointed and dreamlike, but after a series of reverses, he sweeps to
victory with the help of "a bunch of nice cleancut cutthroats,"
who represent the principal military powers of 1939, and among
whom he does not distinguish either as to intent or moral justifica-
tion. With the victory won and the prisoners slaughtered, the
narrator turns to the girl over whom the war has been fought and
whom he has been describing as if he were a lovesick romantic.
The surprise when he cheerfully accepts her degradation and looks
forward to a profitable life as her pimp suddenly refocuses the
emotion of the poem. With this final development the poem be-
comes an allegory of the war economy and the profit motive, as
well as a raging indictment of both the exploitation of sexual love
and humanity's willingness to prostitute its better nature. Its
strength lies in Patchen's use of parody and narrative empathy to

appeal to trite notions of heroism and decency, luring the reader to an abrupt recognition of the motives behind modern warfare.

The success of such poetry depends upon the ability of the Whitmanian artist to identify with the humanity he describes, as much with the tormentors as with the victims. That same ability permits the poet to evoke a sense of almost unlimited reference from his vision of the unity of all life and apply it to his protest—as Patchen does in "The Fox," where the hunter's cruelty is organically part of the crime that kills a soldier, "because there are no dimensions in death." Patchen's deeply felt compassion, his ability to give of himself almost to the point of becoming another, and his feeling for the greater life which dignifies all men and women, save his many identities from being merely personae. Especially when he bends his expansive Whitmanian voice to unadorned moral statement, as he does in "Nice Day For a Lynching," he creates a protest that seems almost inevitably right in its conjunction of personal straightforwardness and collective anguish:

> I don't know this black man.
> I don't know these white men.
>
> But I know that one of my hands
> Is black, and one white. I know that
> One part of me is being strangled,
> While another part horribly laughs.
>
> Until it changes,
> I shall be forever killing; and be killed.

The uncompromising standard by which Patchen operates in these violent poems—that anything that harms anyone is wrong—has, of course, its spiritual as well as its physical application. In fact, the murderous exploitation that debases history is in large part the result of that root crime which, by attacking the imagination, violates the innocence that is the true human nature. This version of the protest theme characterizes much of Patchen's work after World War II. In "When We Were Here Together," for example, Patchen makes probably his most direct protest against the fear that persuades people that their nature is soiled by an original sin and that they must defend themselves against their own kind. The prose-poem opens with a lyric celebration of the innocence of childhood, but quickly turns to an angry denunciation of the social conspiracy that destroys the child's natural sense of self:

> From the beginning they lied. To the child, telling him
> that there was somewhere anger against him, and a hatred
> against him, and only for the reason of his being in the
> world. . . .
>
> And they told the child to starve and to kill the
> child that was within him; for only by doing this could
> he safely enter their world; . . .

As a result of such socialization the child becomes the crippled animal that has traditionally been mistaken for adult—"a thing that had neither the character of a man nor the character of a child, but was a horrible and monstrous parody of the two"—who then goes forth to perpetuate the system from which he received his identity.

The child's experience is reenacted by the narrator of "The Orange Bears," but with reference to a specific milieu. The magic animals "with soft friendly eyes/ Who played with me when I was ten" embody the imaginative world of childhood that is destroyed by the excretions of American capitalism:

> Orange bears with their coats all stunk up with soft coal
> And the National Guard coming over
> From Wheeling to stand in front of the millgates
> With drawn bayonets jeering at the strikers.

The retrospective look at our industrial wasteland, the image, for instance, of the soot settling on the daisies so that "you couldn't tell what they were anymore," reinforces Patchen's rage at the system that corrupts childhood before it can defend its natural consciousness—"A hell of a fat chance my orange bears had!"

As protest, Patchen's prose fictions do not differ dramatically in technique from his poetry, but because of their more extensive development they invite comparison to the realistic or naturalistic

American novels of protest which characterized the Great Depression years when he began his work. His integration of the authorial person into the specific elements of his story is more than a theoretical concern; it also marks an ambitious attempt to engage the reader. Especially because the material of *The Journal of Albion Moonlight*, *Memoirs of a Shy Pornographer*, and *Sleepers Awake* is rarely anything other than the perceptions of the author-narrator, the reader is necessarily involved in locating both the setting of the protest and its emotion. In contrast, what might be called the traditional American protest fiction (by protest fiction I mean novels that make a statement about the plight of relatively helpless, innocent individuals in relation to institutions) generally adopts a point of view far removed from the situation itself, attempts, as it were, to analyze its material from above. Because the author wishes to demonstrate the pressure upon people of forces they do not understand, both he and his audience know more than the characters do about the causality and significance of their lives. The Joads of John Steinbeck's *The Grapes of Wrath* and the crowd of ultimately ineffectual characters who wander through the pages of Frank Norris's *The Octopus* are equally valid examples of people who are initiated into a cyclic process of discovering social law that finally leaves them less enlightened than their reader-observers. It seems almost a formal requirement of protest fiction that its characters be victims of forces to which the readers are not equally subjected, and the emotion we tend to feel for the Joads and similar characters is pity, with its implicit condescension, rather than true compassion. Writers who use this method for a didactic purpose assume that intellectual understanding of the causes of injustice will create a personal involvement in the demand for social change.

In Patchen's work, however, the Everyman whose point of view we are asked to share is also the victim, and we are forced to see things through the victim's eyes if for no other reason than because it is the only way we can understand them. We see no more of the causality of an injustice than the victim himself does; we see only results. Patchen would not expose us, as Frank Norris does, to an elaborate analysis of the American financial practice that kills so many characters in *The Octopus*. He would rather ask us to die in our imaginations with them, only hinting at the institutional logic that determined our fate. This stubborn loyalty to the victim's point of view, which is one source of the obscurity of *The Journal of Albion Moonlight* and *Sleepers Awake*, can be seen operating in the chapter of *Memoirs of a Shy Pornographer* called "House of the Frowning Heart." Here, Albert Budd is lured into a labyrinthian building where he is removed from the transcendent timelessness he had created in his love affair with Priscilla and returned to time as a social apparatus. The "House" of the title represents society and its institutions, which operate without explanation, oppressing Albert for reasons and by methods which he does not understand. He wanders, for instance, into a situation suddenly reminiscent of Catholic confessional practice, which is exemplary of all religions:

> I walked into the booth. It was too dark in there to see much of anything, but I heard something breathing on the other side of a latticed partition. It was just light enough to see that I was supposed to kneel on a stool beside the tiny, window-like opening. After a voice said: "Well?" I said: "I hope you can tell me how to get out of this place. It's terribly important that I catch a train. . . . The woman I love is waiting there for me to carry her off. . . ." "I see," it said slowly. "You plan to make this woman your wife. Have you . . . uh, ever had impure thoughts of her? Have you ever pictured in the cesspool of your mind . . . uh, actions which are not calculated to advance what we may term . . . uh, the spiritual—as opposed to the basely carnal?" (198)

The refusal of the inhuman voice behind the partition to respond to Albert's needs, its insistence on performing its ritual whether relevant or not, is one example of the institution that develops its own will, distinct from and often hostile to the will of the individuals it has been established to serve. There are many more such institutions in the "House of the Frowning Heart." Scarcely is Albert out of the confessional before: "The next thing I saw was a group of men in white smocks standing beside an operating table. 'You're next,' one of them said to me. That seemed to touch off a spring in the others because before I could more than yell a half dozen times I found myself strapped down breathing into a little cloth cup that smelled like a piece of fudge looks" (201).

Albert's misadventures in the Kafkaesque house probably represent the helplessness of innocence in a culture organized according to power. In any case, the reason for the horribly impersonal tortures he endures is never explained, and probably does not exist in any rational sense. The uncertainty is typical of all Patchen's protest writing. Instead of being offered a coherent analysis of what has gone wrong in the world, we are returned to the irrevocable origins of protest: the emotional knowledge that man is in pain. If the technique is not so effective for teaching purposes as that adopted in more familiar proletarian and naturalistic novels, it is more actively engaged with the raw material of life under oppression.

Patchen's protest writing has probably been overemphasized by his critics, whose emphases have made the bulk of his controversial work seem relatively larger than it is. His great rage and uninhibited techniques have sometimes taken flight in a rhetoric that has earned him a reputation as offensive and irresponsible. The reputation is not entirely unmerited. He certainly has proved capable of truly appalling lapses of taste and decorum. Despite such problems, much of Patchen's protest stands up after four decades and more, primarily because of his personal compassion and magnanimity. He comes with the bark on, but he expresses a kind of cranky goodness that ennobles both his work and the reader who enters it. In an introduction to the sometimes ranting anger of Allen Ginsberg's *Howl*, William Carlos Williams remarked that "Poets are damned but they are not blind,"[18] and Kenneth Patchen, more than Ginsberg, bears witness to the observation. His unflinching respect for the responsibilities of his art is illustrated in "Behold, One of Several Little Christs," in the description of the modern crucifixion that might well be his terse explanation of an entire career:

> Nail her to the door my leader said and they put knives
> Through her hands and knives through her feet, but
> I did not turn my face away
> *I am a singer of songs and there is no one*
> *Listening now*

Epilogue

But ah, alas, sooner or later each of us
must stand before that grim Roman Court
          —Patchen, "O She Is as Lovely-Often as Every Day"

After years of keeping track of Patchen's public fortunes I still consider his literary reputation with some impatience, less because the common judgment about him has been adverse than because it has not been rigorously made at all. Both popular and professional opinion concerning Patchen has been largely a creature of the weather, rising and falling on winds of relevancy, unleashed usually by partisan responses to isolated aspects of the work. Except for such recent beginnings as Larry R. Smith's volume in the Twayne United States Authors series and the anthologizing of Richard Morgan, there have been no attempts to describe and assess Patchen's full range of achievement. Consequently, he has remained marginal and perhaps a little ghostly, like some wild orphan, some surly American Heathcliffe, forever beating against windows that are locked against him, abandoned to his own world of shadow and storm.

His death was noticed in the national press, but it provoked no important critical statement either there or in eminent literary periodicals. Such media had never had much to say about him. The obituaries listed his credits and his few awards, generally according him the cautious respect due a man who had gone down fighting the good fight in a suspect cause. Responses from the artistic and bohemian community, of course, were warmer and more spirited. Undoubtedly their most ambitious expression was the memorial reading that a number of poets, led by Al Young, organized in San Francisco in February 1972. Richard Hack has published a lively, sometimes moving account of the activity on what was apparently a memorable evening. Lawrence Ferlinghetti read his "An Elegy on the Death of Kenneth Patchen" and there were tributes by Robert Duncan, Gary Snyder, and Robert Creeley, among a host of other writers, both well known and obscure. Despite a few incidents which might have led Patchen, who had always been suspicious of such occasions, to energize his "built-in, foolproof, shock-proof shit detector," the gathering seems to have been chiefly moved by unrehearsed affection and admiration, and a genuine sense of loss.[1]

Poets turned out in numbers that evening because they had been called to take leave of a colleague they considered both exemplary and heroic. Especially during the last years of his life, when Vietnam was on everybody's mind, Patchen's long-standing reputation for moral outspokenness and refusal to compromise had made him a symbol of resistance. For an extended historical moment he was to many novices in protest the incarnation of the scarred old rebel, the father of dissent and champion of causes forever sacred to the young. At the height of antidraft and other pacifist movements, war-resisters David Harris and Joan Baez had been married in a ceremony that included Patchen's poem of 1939, "The Character of Love Seen as a Search for the Lost," with its urgency and challenges:

> Have you wondered why all the windows in heaven were
> broken?
> Have you seen the homeless in the open grave of God's hand?
> Do you want to acquaint the larks with the fatuous music of
> war?

But the timely outcries of the Vietnam years passed, as timely outcries will, and Patchen's inflexible pacifism and hatred of collaboration in themselves can no longer keep his name or work current.

The poem by which Baez and Harris announced their stand reflects not only Patchen's social concern, but also the other major component of his popular reputation, one that has survived better during the decade after his death. Direct, unironic, unembarrassed affirmations of the transcendent qualities of romantic love claimed a special ideological and emotional significance for him, and he persistently composed a great many of them. The fear of being sentimental, he thought, was a sign of decadence. Since 1948 there have been several volumes of selections from Patchen's verse that have consisted exclusively, or nearly so, of love lyrics.[2] Two of them, commercially illustrated, were issued as inexpensive giftbooks by the Hallmark Card Company. Hallmark also distributed at least one greeting card, a sentimentalized pastoral, which reprinted part of "What There Is" from *When We Were Here Together*.

As "The Character of Love Seen as a Search for the Lost" demonstrates, Patchen can be a significant love poet, particularly when he expresses the tension between love and the violent, corrupt culture in which it must be expressed. He has made some remarkably fresh contributions to a genre which traditionally resists innovation. The popular taste for his love lyrics, however, seems to have developed not so much despite as because of the sentimentality and conventionality of many of his least successful efforts. It may well be that "23rd Street Runs Into Heaven" is his single most popular poem. Those fashionably garish Hallmark cards and books, unnerving as Patchen's defenders may find them, reflect the degree to which the love poetry has comprised almost a separate career, free of the recriminations and dismissals that have attended the controversial writing, but without any substantial literary audience. As a sentimentalist, Patchen has attracted a small number of the readers who made bestsellers of Kahlil Gibran, Walter Benton, and Rod McKuen. In fact, the correspondence is close enough that there has developed a sort of folklore about the authorship of the pseudonymous Benton's *This Is My Beloved*, a dexterous book of vapidities which enjoyed large sales for many years. I have been told seriously on several occasions either that Patchen got drunk at a party and wrote *This Is My Beloved* in an evening or that he and Kenneth Fearing got drunk and wrote it together. A friend of Patchen's discovered a version of the story circulating in Ohio as early as 1950.[3] These uncritical recognitions and associations and the exaggerated applause that accompanies them may constitute, finally, a defeat of Patchen's literary status far more destructive than anything visited on him by the most virulent new critic.

Beyond such essentially tangential attention, there has been little in recent years to keep Patchen's name alive. Some interest in his painting was sparked by an exhibit at the Corcoran Gallery in Washington, D.C., in 1969–70, shortly before his death, but he worked in small, eccentric media, such as decorated books, and his paintings are so widely scattered that it is all but impossible for individuals to see any substantial number of them. In any case, apart from poem-paintings the plastic arts were an avocation, and Patchen himself did not much emphasize his achievement in them.[4]

As material became available after Patchen's death, Richard Morgan undertook the important bibliographical record and collection of fugitive pieces. Once his work and Larry Smith's book are acknowledged, Patchen's remaining currency rests largely on the continuing interest of the small, loyal readership he has always attracted, especially among the idealists who sustain small presses and little magazines, the young, and collectors of first editions, who keep his original titles both scarce and expensive. His influence is alive too, particularly on the West Coast, but because of his markedly personal idiom, which was difficult even for him to sustain without awkwardness, it has been essentially a moral influence and only incidentally stylistic.

Part of Patchen's inaccessibility to comprehensive questions of judgment is due to his own guff and crankiness. He stridently resisted identification, and hence comparability, with writers in the mainstream of modernist literature, and his moral stance frequently made his work difficult to examine properly. It is not easy to be dispassionate about a man who has his finger stuck in your chest. Further, he was downright abusive about suggestions as to national or regional literary affiliations. If in some interesting world he could read this Americanist study of mine and find himself compared extensively to Walt Whitman, he might have some pretty brisk remarks for me. A raucous poem from the early 1940s called "Hell Gate Bridge" sums up his attitudes toward American literary nationalism. The title, of course, refers mockingly to Hart Crane's celebration of Brooklyn Bridge, and the poem hoots at the cultural nationalists (among them the later Van Wyck Brooks and Lewis Mumford) who chase their "tri-motored myth" the length of "the Mississippi,/ The Yazoo, the Chippewa, the Gunnisoh" and through the symbolic Hell Gate to "our American Eden," where "on the bosom of Jeff Davis the Tates throb."[5]

So I claim him as a traditional American writer despite himself, not so much for what he says about such things as for the way he goes about saying them, and I think that it would be both sad and wasteful if American letters were to refuse the heritage of his astringent presence. Making predictions is a fool's game, but harmless enough, and it seems to me at least plausible to hope that Patchen's reputation will follow the pattern, even though it will never approach the stature, of Whitman's. In the critical neglect he suffered, the traumatic experience of war, and the physical disorder which crippled him, Patchen's life developed strange parallels to his spiritual ancestor's. It requires only a little imagination to speculate that he will continue to resemble Whitman by being recognized at some future time as a distinctly American artist, but one who is always suspect, a disturber of the peace.

That would be honorable, but it is not much to offer a good poet. In our beloved community we would do better for our prophets, gadflies, and other compulsively honest people.

Notes

Preface

1. Anonymous, undated reader's report of 1972 to the University of Wisconsin Press.

2. Patchen, "A Mercy-Filled & Defiant Xmas To All Still Worthy To Be Called Men," privately published broadside poem, [1970]. The calligraphic text was reproduced in color in *Mano-Mano* 2 (1971): 63–64.

3. Patchen, *Collected Poems*, p. 103.

4. Useful biographical chronologies may be found in Morgan, *Kenneth Patchen: A Collection of Essays*, pp. xiii–xvi; and Smith, *Kenneth Patchen*, unnumbered pp. 13–16.

5. See, for example, Smith, *Patchen*, in the only book-length study of Patchen yet published.

6. The friend was Mrs. Joel Climenhaga, whose husband told me about the incident in 1967.

7. The remainder of the preface is in part a distillation of my "Mysticism and the Problems of Mystical Literature," pp. 1–26.

8. See Katz, "Language, Epistemology, and Mysticism," pp. 22–74, for a rigorous insistence on the differences in mystical experience. See Stace, *Mysticism and Philosophy*, pp. 41–47, for the most influential recent assertions about the commonality of mystical experience.

9. Ben-Ami Scharfstein's suggestion that humor is one of the quintessential characteristics of mysticism is undoubtedly eccentric, but it is also insightful. See Scharfstein, *Mystical Experience*, p. 166.

10. The supersensory quality of mysticism is definitive for some commentators. See, for instance, Jones, *Some Exponents of Mystical Religion*, p. 15.

11. For both omniscience and ineffability see James, *Varieties of Religious Experience*, pp. 380–81. Other valuable discussions of the controversial question of ineffability include Stace, *Mysticism and Philosophy*, pp. 277–306; and Organ, "The Language of Mysticism," pp. 417–43.

12. Inge, *Christian Mysticism*, p. 5. See also Stace, *Mysticism and*

Philosophy, p. 343; and Staal, *Exploring Mysticism*, p. 190. For a Jungian application of the attitude see Neumann, "Mystical Man," pp. 375–415.

13. See, for instance, Inge, *Christian Mysticism*, p. 28; James, *Varieties of Religious Experience*, p. 408; Underhill, *Mysticism*, pp. 26, 87; and Zaehner, *Mysticism Sacred and Profane*, p. 144.

14. See Underhill's discussion of the unitive state, *Mysticism*, pp. 413–43.

15. I take this term from the insistence on the sensory qualities of conversion in Jonathan Edwards's "Personal Narrative," and from Underhill, *Mysticism*, p. 242.

16. See Underhill, *Mysticism*, pp. 415–43.

17. See the discussion by Govinda in *Foundations of Tibetan Mysticism*, pp. 129–31.

18. James, *Varieties of Religious Experience*, p. 426. See also Stace, *Mysticism and Philosophy*, p. 163, on the plenum-vacuum paradox of mysticism.

19. The best discussion of madness in mystical literature is Fowlie, *Clowns and Angels*, pp. 130–46. See also Underhill, *Mysticism*, 58–65; and Ben-Ami Scharfstein's chapter on "Psychotic Mysticism," in *Mystical Experience*, pp. 133–40.

20. Staal, *Exploring Mysticism*, p. 150.

21. Royce, *The World and the Individual*, p. 81.

22. See Underhill, *Mysticism*, pp. 429–31; Staal, *Exploring Mysticism*, pp. 141–42; Stace, *Mysticism and Philosophy*, pp. 323–43; Crastre, *Poesie et Mystique*, p. 40; Leuba, *The Psychology of Religious Mysticism*, pp. 62–63; and Ghose, *Mystics and Society*.

23. The story is included in Reps's *Zen Flesh, Zen Bones*, p. 34.

24. In Happold, *Mysticism*, p. 323.

25. Quoted in Watts, *The Spirit of Zen*, p. 52.

26. Legge, *The Texts of Taoism*, 1:198–200.

27. I have paraphrased Legge's somewhat too literal and awkward translation, which reads: "He who knows (the Tao) does not (care to) speak (about it); he who is (ever ready to) speak about it does not know it." The first of the passages from the *Tao Te Ching* used in this paragraph is from Legge, *Texts of Taoism*, 1:47; and the second from 1:100.

28. Quoted in Reps, *Zen Flesh, Zen Bones*, p. 127.

29. I have borrowed this observation from Morris, "Mysticism and Its Language," pp. 179–87. See also Stace, *Mysticism and Philosophy*, pp. 277–306; Organ, "Language of Mysticism"; and Moore, "Mystical Experience, Mystical Doctrine, Mystical Technique," pp. 101–31.

30. Quoted in Morris, "Mysticism and Its Language," p. 180.

31. See Ewer, *A Survey of Mystical Symbolism*.

32. Saint John of the Cross [Juan de Yepes], *Complete Works*, 2:24.

33. I discuss the case of the *I Ching* in some detail in "Mysticism and the Problems of Mystical Literature," pp. 21–26.

34. See Sanders, "Zen Buddhism and the Japanese Haiku," 4:211–17.

35. Henry Miller, *Tropic of Capricorn*, p. 40.

Chapter 1

1. For this, and much of the other discussion of early Puritan mysticism, see Maclear, " 'Heart of New England Rent,' " pp. 621–52.

2. See Perry Miller, *Errand into the Wilderness*, pp. 184–203.

3. Jacoby, *Le Mysticisme dans le Pensée Américaine*. The only other full study of mysticism in the United States is *American Mysticism from William James to Zen* by Leonard Hal Bridges.

4. They are an important subject for Bridges, *American Mysticism*, and his is the fullest account.

5. See Astro, "Steinbeck and Ricketts," pp. 24–33.

6. For the young Van Wyck Brooks's affiliation with American literary mysticism see my *Van Wyck Brooks*, pp. 84–150.

7. Most readers will probably accept my suggestion about Whitman, Miller, Roethke, and Patchen as a working hypothesis, but may stumble over Williams, who went out of his way to appear hardheaded and commonsensical. Williams's own testimony, however, was given in a letter to Marianne Moore of 2 May 1934: "It is something that occurred once when I was about twenty, a sudden resignation to existence, a despair—if you wish to call it that, but a despair which made everything a unit and at the same time a part of myself. I suppose it might be called a sort of nameless religious experience. . . . I won't follow causes. I can't. The reason is that it seems so much more important to me that I *am.* . . . As a reward for this anonymity I feel as much a part of things as trees and stones" (Williams, *The Selected Letters of William Carlos Williams*, p. 147).

8. See, for example, Whitman's *Democratic Vistas* in *Prose Works 1892*, 2:361–425, and any of the invocatory poems; the discussions of the complete man in Henry Miller, *The Colossus of Maroussi*; Brooks, *America's Coming-of-Age*, p. 39; Bittner, *The Novels of Waldo Frank*, p. 23; Bucke, *Cosmic Consciousness*; and the works of Ralph Waldo Emerson.

9. Trueblood, "The fullness of the Godhead dwelt in every blade of grass," pp. 332–34.

10. I have used the translation by Prabhavananda and Manchester, *The Upanishads*, p. 18.

11. Holland, *Essays and a Drama*, p. 105.

12. Blyth, *Zen in English Literature and Oriental Classics*, p. 403.

13. See Bridges, *American Mysticism*, pp. 97–99.

14. J. Hillis Miller, *Poets of Reality*, p. 287.

15. Williams, *Spring and All*, p. 121.

16. Quoted in Watts, *The Way of Zen*, p. 127.

17. Charles I. Glicksberg has studied surrealism as a fraudulent mysticism in "Mysticism in Contemporary Poetry," pp. 233–45. In the same article Glicksberg considers Patchen a true mystical artist.

18. I owe much of my knowledge of Patchen's reading to the kindness of Joel Climenhaga, who permitted me to read many of his unpublished letters to Patchen, and whose enthusiastic conversations about Patchen have helped me mightily.

19. Williams, "America, Whitman, and the Art of Poetry," p. 31.

20. For a discussion of the relationship between karma and compensation, see Christy, *The Orient in American Transcendentalism*, pp. 98–104.

21. Saint John of the Cross, *Complete Works*, 1:x.

22. Cowley, in his introduction to his reissue of the 1855 edition of *Leaves of Grass*, pp. xxvi–xxxii.

23. Winters, *In Defense of Reason*, pp. 575–603.

24. Perry Miller, *Errand into the Wilderness*, p. 185.

25. Brooks, *America's Coming-of-Age*, pp. 114–19.

26. Cowley, introduction to *Leaves of Grass*, pp. xxxiii–xxxiv.

27. Again, this idea may be less familiar in Williams than in the others. See the chapter called "Of Medicine and Poetry" in Williams, *The Autobiography of William Carlos Williams*, pp. 286–89.

28. Chase, *Walt Whitman Reconsidered*, pp. 58–98.

Chapter 2

1. Merton, *The Ascent to Truth*, pp. 61–62. Bonnie Bowman Thurston reminded me of the existence of this useful passage.

2. Merton, *The Sign of Jonas*, p. 244.

3. See, for instance, Andreach, *Studies in Structure*, pp. 6–7. Andreach also describes the five-fold way first identified by Evelyn Under-

hill, with which Patchen has displayed his familiarity. Either system might have been applied to Patchen, but the tripartite has the virtue of requiring less ingenuity of application and less attention to explaining the system itself.

4. Page references to the volumes under discussion will be included in parentheses in the text.

5. Eckman, "The Comic Apocalypse of Kenneth Patchen," pp. 389–92.

6. In *Collected Poems* Patchen retitled this piece "Prayer *Not* to Go to Paradise with the Asses" (my emphasis). I am not sure I know why.

7. For a socialist critique of *Before the Brave* see Lozar, "*Before the Brave*," pp. 193–207.

8. Wilder, *Spiritual Aspects of the New Poetry*, pp. 178–95.

9. Underhill, *Mysticism*, p. 10.

10. Fowlie, *Clowns and Angels*, p. 182.

11. Patchen, "Bury Them in God," pp. 128–44.

12. One good comparison between Whitman and Patchen appears in Taylor, "Puck in the Gardens of the Sun," pp. 269–74.

13. Whitman, *Prose Works 1892*, 2:424.

14. Lawrence, *Studies in Classic American Literature*. See especially the essays on James Fenimore Cooper and Edgar Allan Poe.

15. For a discussion of Patchen's concrete poetry, see Smith, *Kenneth Patchen*, pp. 113–24.

16. According to Miriam Patchen (letter to author, June 1969), the books of this transitional time were composed in the following order: *Pictures of Life and of Death* and *They Keep Riding Down All the Time* (about simultaneously), *Panels for the Walls of Heaven*, *Memoirs of a Shy Pornographer*, *Sleepers Awake*, and *See You in the Morning*.

17. Miriam Patchen to author, 23 December 1966.

18. This poem-painting is reproduced in color in Patchen, *The Argument of Innocence*, p. 50. There is a murky black and white reproduction in Patchen, *Wonderings*, an unpaged volume.

19. Eckman, "Comic Apocalypse," pp. 390–91.

Chapter 3

1. Kennedy, review of *Cloth of the Tempest*; and Lazarus, review of *Cloth of the Tempest*, p. 80.

2. Fiedler, introduction to *Whitman*, pp. 8–9.

3. E. Fred Carlisle's concept of the "dialogal" aspect of Whitman's

sense of identity is a useful corrective to the common description of Whitman in Emersonian terms. See Carlisle, *The Uncertain Self*.

4. Parenthetical page references in the text are to Whitman, *Prose Works 1892*.

5. For Whitman's access to German philosophy see Stovall, *The Foreground of Leaves of Grass*, pp. 194–96. For the American Hegelians and their concept of identity see Goetzmann, introduction to his *The American Hegelians*, pp. 3–18.

6. Rauch, *Psychology*, p. 4. Further page references will be cited in the text. I am obliged to John McVeigh for alerting me to the existence of this document.

7. See, for instance, Whitman, "To a Pupil," in the third edition of *Leaves of Grass*, p. 400.

8. Wilson's review and Miller's reply are reprinted in Wilson, *The Shores of Light*, pp. 705–10.

9. Patchen, *The Journal of Albion Moonlight*, p. 22. Further page references will be cited in the text. All editions of this book have the same pagination.

10. Brooks, *The Malady of the Ideal*, pp. 34–36. For Brooks on the romantic dilemma of the conflict between poetry and form, see my *Van Wyck Brooks*, pp. 72–88.

11. A rough skeleton of the main forms and digressions in the narrative follows: pp. 1–57: the original journal; pp. 57–156: the original journal and the first of Albion's novels alternate with one another; p. 156: the second novel begins, and continues to p. 168 (it is also part of the first novel); pp. 160–63: a second journal, with parallel entries for 2 May–15 June (it is part of the second novel); p. 163: the third novel (a one-page fragment explicitly about the violation of the girl-child); p. 168: return to the first novel; p. 169: return to the first journal, which continues to p. 268; pp. 179–83: a double narrative of historical violence (the text) and the violation of the girl-child (the margin), both of which are set in a medieval age, and are more of Albion's fictions as part of the first journal; pp. 216–57: as part of his journal, Albion includes his "Notes," which are fragments of his experience and thinking which have not been worked into any of the novels or journals—this section becomes a kind of long Whitmanian poem interposed with scraps of nonfiction, catalogues, and some important narrative material, including (pp. 249–52) the account of Albion's death; p. 257: return to the first journal; p. 268: the first journal "ends" at 17 August (this is a red herring—the journal picks up again later); pp. 269–81: the "Notes" again; p. 281: the original novel again, a variant of chapter 14, and it is important to cross-reference it with the original (p. 140); pp. 282–95: the

tables of contents of two novels, both part of the text of the first novel; pp. 304–6: "The Little Journal"—parallel entries for 2 and 3 May; and, p. 306 to end: the original journal. Morgan has elaborated this outline in "*The Journal of Albion Moonlight*," pp. 176–78.

12. Henry Miller, *The Wisdom of the Heart*, p. 24.

13. Williams, *The Collected Earlier Poems*, p. 166.

14. Eliot, *The Use of Poetry and the Use of Criticism*, p. 144.

Chapter 4

1. Rexroth, *Bird in the Bush*, p. 103. Additional commentary on this aspect of Patchen's work may be found in Henry Miller, *Patchen*, which was reprinted in *Stand Still Like the Hummingbird*; and in McGovern, "Kenneth Patchen's Prose Works," pp. 189–97.

2. Henry Miller, *Wisdom of the Heart*, p. 28.

3. Stevens, "William Carlos Williams," p. 63.

4. Williams, *I Wanted to Write a Poem*, p. 52.

5. Ibid., p. 18.

6. David Gascoyne, introduction to *Outlaw of the Lowest Planet* by Kenneth Patchen, p. x.

7. Le Maître, *From Cubism to Surrealism in French Literature*, pp. 197–99.

8. Cf. Rexroth, *Bird in the Bush*, p. 104: "Patchen must be distinguished from the later, orthodox Surrealists. This stuff was largely a dreamy rehash of the troubles of rich women and their favorites of the literary, artistic, and pathic international. Rare, unhappy schoolboys here and there around the world may have read Breton once with excitement, but it takes modistes, comtesses, and American heiresses to read him with understanding."

9. Taylor, "Puck in the Gardens of the Sun," pp. 269–74.

10. The novel includes pages 67–87, 103–16, 126–62, 184–88, 188–209 (this sequence is actually a novel-within-a-novel which, although part of the first novel, does nothing to advance the main action), 361–65, and 376–81.

Chapter 5

1. Williams, *I Wanted to Write a Poem*, pp. 73–74.

2. Steinbeck, *The Log from the Sea of Cortez*, p. 1.

3. Henry Miller, *The Wisdom of the Heart*, pp. 22, 23, and 28.

4. Patchen, *Journal of Albion Moonlight*, p. 245. Further page references for Patchen's books will be included in the text.

5. See Underhill, *Mysticism*, pp. 167–75 and throughout. Underhill's great contribution was to distinguish this more psychologically accurate model from the three-fold division of patristic Christianity.

6. Patchen, "Blake," second page of an unnumbered introduction. Patchen may have taken his outline directly from Underhill, or from S. Foster Damon, whose *William Blake, His Philosophy and Symbols* he had read and admired. I am not aware of a source (if there was one) for the secondary five-fold breakdown he offers.

7. Cowley, introduction to *Leaves of Grass*, pp. vi–xxxvii. James E. Miller, Jr., *A Critical Guide to Leaves of Grass*, pp. 6–35.

8. Chari, *Whitman in the Light of Vedantic Mysticism*, pp. 122–27.

9. I am basing my remarks on Cowley's issue of the first edition here, and line numbers refer to his arrangement. There were, of course, no divisions into sections in 1855, but because Whitman added them later it would be a wasteful sort of purism not to take advantage of them.

10. Further examples of this imagery (besides Patchen's usage, which will be discussed later) can be found in Williams's *Paterson* I, i; Henry Miller, *Tropic of Capricorn*, p. 329; and the unpublished notebooks of the young Van Wyck Brooks (see my *Van Wyck Brooks*, pp. 62–63). Chari, in *Whitman* (pp. 76–77), has a valuable discussion of the image:

> "The self which says, 'they are not the Me myself,' which witnesses and waits while the endless spectacle of the world goes by, and which retains its identity in the midst of the shifting processes is the transcendental witness in us, of which the scriptures speak. The poet who wanders all night in his vision, dreaming all the dreams of the other dreamers, who traverses the whole span of the universe, becoming by turns the bride, the bridegroom, the hounded slave, and 'the sleepless widow looking out on the winter midnight' is the self as *saksi* or the detached percipience. The Upanishads describe two birds perching on a tree, one of which feeds on the delicious fruit, while the other, not tasting of it looks on. The one is the empirical subject, the other the perpetual percipient which sees but does not enjoy. The Gita speaks of the supreme self in the body which is the witness, permitter, supporter and the experiencer. 'He appears to have the qualities of all the senses, and yet is without the senses, *unattached* yet *supporting all, free from the dispositions of Prakriti and yet enjoying them*.' Though participating in the world action this self is unfettered. According to the Upanishads, 'After enjoying himself and roaming, and merely see-

ing good and evil, he stays in a state of profound sleep and comes back to his former condition. Whatever he sees there he is untouched by it, for this infinite being is unattached.' This consciousness of distinction between his real nature or 'soul' and the phenomenal strata of his mind is constant in Whitman."

11. See "Hart Crane" in Andreach, *Studies in Structure*, pp. 102–29. Andreach's argument tends to make Crane's sequence tidier and more premeditated than it is. *The Bridge* seems to be a confused amalgam of several forms, none of which emerges as definitive.

12. See Trismosin, *Splendor Solis*. The first picture on the walls of heaven is adapted from Plate 5; the third from Plate 9; the fourth from Plate 10; the fifth from Plate 22; and the seventh from Plate 17.

13. Eckman, "Comic Apocalypse," pp. 389–92.

Chapter 6

1. Both passages are from Patchen, "from 'A Note on *The Hunted City*,'" p. 69.

2. Moreover, the strategies for dealing with free verse that have been developed over the past two decades (usually with specific reference to the works of individual poets) have essentially adapted and applied the capabilities of traditional metric prosody. See, for instance, Hartman's delightful and revealing analysis of Marianne Moore's "Bird-Witted" in his *Free Verse*, pp. 19–20.

3. Chase, *Walt Whitman Reconsidered*, p. 9.

4. See Cary Nelson, *Our Last First Poets*, pp. 97–101.

5. Cf. Hartman, *Free Verse*, p. 81, for the "special community" between the maker and "user" of a poem in free verse.

6. Levertov, "Some Notes on Organic Form," pp. 141–45.

7. Patchen, *Collected Poems*, p. 22. Examples of Patchen's verse in this chapter may all be found in *Collected Poems*.

8. Patchen, "from 'A Note on *The Hunted City*," p. 69.

9. Barney Childs discusses both "What Is the Beautiful?" and "The Murder of Two Men by a Young Kid Wearing Lemon-colored Gloves" as notations by which a poem is read in time in "Articulation in Sound Structure," pp. 423–45.

Chapter 7

1. Just as a sampling of this attitude among both hostile and sympathetic reviewers, see: Walton, review of *First Will & Testament*; Breit, "On a Bronze Horse," pp. 160–63; Warren, review of *The Dark Kingdom*, p. 17; Schwartz, "'I Feel Drunk All the Time,'" pp. 220, 222; Untermeyer, "Problem of Patchen," pp. 15–16; and Eckman, "Comic Apocalypse," pp. 89–92.

2. Chaplin, *Wobbly*, p. 38.

3. Ginger, *The Bending Cross*, pp. 231–32.

4. Chase, *Walt Whitman Reconsidered*, pp. 153–65.

5. Brooks, *America's Coming-of-Age*, p. 33.

6. For a more detailed account of *America's Coming-of-Age* and Brooks's adaptation of Whitmanian methods, see my *Van Wyck Brooks*, pp. 100–108, 293–96.

7. Frank, *The Re-Discovery of America*, p. 24. Further page references will be included in the text.

8. Williams, *In the American Grain*, unpaged preface. Page references will be included in the text.

9. Henry Miller, *The Air-Conditioned Nightmare*, p. 26. Further page references will be included in the text.

10. Henry Miller, *Remember to Remember*, p. 47.

11. Steinbeck, *Sea of Cortez* (New York, 1941). The narrative portion was later excerpted and published as *The Log from the Sea of Cortez*. Page references in the text are to the *Log* because it is much more readily accessible than the original study. Because of the collaboration, it is often difficult to attribute particular passages and attitudes directly to Steinbeck. Many of the philosophical and scientific ideas, especially monistic ones, were Ricketts's, although the division was never sharp and clear. In my discussion, I have pretty much ignored such important matters and conventionally attributed everything in the *Log* to Steinbeck. He organized and rewrote the material, and was willing to put his name to it upon republication after Ricketts's death. Also, even ideas he might have wished to modify are consistent with and can help illuminate his own incipient nature mysticism in such early books as *To A God Unknown*. For these reasons it has seemed to me unnecessary to try to sort ideas out or to invent a composite Steinbeck/Ricketts. My limited purposes are served primarily by the existence of the book and its perspective rather than by particular attributions. The complex relationship between Steinbeck and Ricketts, and their joint authorship of *Sea of Cortez*, is discussed admirably in Astro, *John Steinbeck and Edward P. Ricketts*.

12. Astro, *Steinbeck and Ricketts*, p. 22.

13. Mumford, *The Conduct of Life*, p. 317. Further page references will be included in the text.

14. For examples of the primacy of the evolutionary future in Brooks's work see my *Van Wyck Brooks*, pp. 86–87, 293.

15. Hill, *The Letters of Joe Hill*, p. 50.

16. Rexroth, *Bird in the Bush*, pp. 95–99.

17. Patchen, *Collected Poems*, p. 196. Other examples of Patchen's verse in this chapter may be found in *Collected Poems*.

18. Williams, introduction to *Howl and Other Poems*, p. 8.

Epilogue

1. Hack, "Memorial Poetry Reading for Kenneth Patchen," pp. 81–97.

2. The volumes are as follows: *To Say If You Love Someone*; *The Love Poems of Kenneth Patchen*; *Love & War Poems, whisper & shout* 1; *There's Love All Day*; and *Tell You That I Love You*.

3. Joel Climenhaga to Kenneth Patchen 27 April and 23 June 1950. Mr. Climenhaga kindly made copies of these letters available to me.

4. See Detro, "Patchen Interviewed," pp. 70–71.

5. The poem appears in *The Teeth of the Lion*, unpaged. It was not reprinted in *Collected Poems*.

Bibliography

I have generally preferred to cite the most readily accessible editions of all authors except Patchen, whose works are listed in their original versions. During the 1960s and 1970s New Directions reissued most of the collections, pamphlets, and fugitive pieces Patchen had earlier published with Padell and other small houses, but the reissues are often typographically so different from the originals that they are in effect different texts.

Andreach, Robert J. *Studies in Structure*. New York: Fordham University Press, 1964.

Astro, Richard. *John Steinbeck and Edward F. Ricketts: The Shaping of A Novelist*. Minneapolis: University of Minnesota Press, 1973.

————. "Steinbeck and Ricketts: The Morphology of a Metaphysic." *University of Windsor Review* 8 (1973): 24–33.

Bittner, William. *The Novels of Waldo Frank*. Philadelphia: University of Pennsylvania Press, 1958.

Blyth, Robert H. *Zen in English Literature and Oriental Classics*. Tokyo: Hokuseido Press, 1942.

Breit, Harvey. "On a Bronze Horse." *Poetry* 40 (1942): 160–63.

Bridges, Leonard Hal. *American Mysticism from William James to Zen*. New York: Harper and Row, 1970.

Brooks, Van Wyck. *America's Coming-of-Age*. New York: B. W. Huebsch, 1915.

————. *The Malady of the Ideal*. Philadelphia: University of Pennsylvania Press, 1947.

Bucke, Richard M. *Cosmic Consciousness*. 5th edition. New York: Dutton, 1926.

Carlisle, E. Fred. *The Uncertain Self: Whitman's Drama of Identity*. N.p.: Michigan State University Press, 1973.

Chaplin, Ralph. *Wobbly: The Rough-and-Tumble Story of an American Radical*. Chicago: University of Chicago Press, 1948.

Chari, V. K. *Whitman in the Light of Vedantic Mysticism*. Lincoln: University of Nebraska Press, 1964.

Chase, Richard. *Walt Whitman Reconsidered*. New York: William Sloane, 1955.

Childs, Barney. "Articulation in Sound Structure: Some Notes toward an Analytic." *Texas Studies in Literature and Language* 8 (1967): 423–45.

Christy, Arthur. *The Orient in American Transcendentalism*. New York: Columbia University Press, 1932.

Cowley, Malcolm. Introduction to *Leaves of Grass: The First (1855) Edition*. New York: Viking, 1959.

Crastre, Victor. *Poesie et Mystique*. Newchatel: La Baconniere, 1966.

Detro, Gene. "Patchen Interviewed." In *Kenneth Patchen: A Collection of Essays*, edited by Richard Morgan, pp. 68–78. New York: AMS Press, 1977.

Eckman, Frederick. "The Comic Apocalypse of Kenneth Patchen." *Poetry* 92 (1958): 389–92.

Edwards, Jonathan. "Personal Narrative." In *Jonathan Edwards*, edited by Clarence H. Faust and Thomas H. Johnson, pp. 57–72. New York: Hill and Wang, 1962.

Eliot, T. S. *The Use of Poetry and the Use of Criticism*. Cambridge: Harvard University Press, 1933.

Emerson, Ralph Waldo. *Works*. Edited by Edward W. Emerson. 12 vols. Boston: Houghton Mifflin Company, 1903–4.

Ewer, Mary Anita. *A Survey of Mystical Symbolism*. New York: Macmillan, 1933.

Fiedler, Leslie, ed. *Whitman*. New York: Dell, 1959.

Fowlie, Wallace. *Clowns and Angels*. New York: Sheed and Ward, 1943.

Frank, Waldo. *Our America*. New York: Boni and Liveright, 1919.
———. *The Re-Discovery of America*. New York: Scribner's, 1929.

Gascoyne, David. Introduction to *Outlaw of the Lowest Planet* by Kenneth Patchen. London: Grey Walls Press, 1946.

Ghose, Sisirkumar. *Mystics and Society: A Point of View*. Bombay: Asia Publishing House, 1968.

Ginger, Ray. *The Bending Cross: A Biography of Eugene Victor Debs*. New Brunswick: Rutgers University Press, 1949.

Ginsberg, Allen. *Howl and Other Poems*. San Francisco: City Lights, 1956.
———. *Kaddish and Other Poems*. San Francisco: City Lights, 1961.

Glicksberg, Charles I. "Mysticism in Contemporary Poetry." *Antioch Review* 3 (1943): 233–45.

Goetzmann, William H. *The American Hegelians: An Intellectual Episode in the History of Western America*. New York: Knopf, 1973.

Govinda, Anagarika. *Foundations of Tibetan Mysticism*. London: Rider and Company, 1969.

Hack, Richard. "Memorial Poetry Reading for Kenneth Patchen." In *Kenneth Patchen: A Collection of Essays*, edited by Richard Morgan, pp. 87–97. New York: AMS Press, 1977.

Happold, F. C. *Mysticism: A Study and An Anthology*. Baltimore: Penguin, 1970.

Hartman, Charles O. *Free Verse: An Essay on Prosody*. Princeton: Princeton University Press, 1980.

Hill, Joe [Joseph Hillstrom]. *The Letters of Joe Hill*. Edited by Philip S. Foner. New York: Oak Publications, 1965.

Holland, E. G. *Essays and a Drama*. Boston: Phillips, Sampson, and Company, 1852.

Inge, W. R. *Christian Mysticism*. New York: Scribner's, 1899.

Jacoby, John E. *Le Mysticisme dans le Penseé Américaine*. Paris: Les Universitaires de France, 1931.

James, William. *The Varieties of Religious Experience*. New York: Longmans, Green and Company, 1902.

Jones, Rufus. *Some Exponents of Mystical Religion*. New York: Abingdon Press, 1930.

Katz, Steven T. "Language, Epistemology, and Mysticism." In *Mysticism and Philosophical Analysis*, edited by Steven T. Katz, pp. 22–74. New York: Oxford University Press, 1978.

Kennedy, Leo. Review of *Cloth of the Tempest*, by Kenneth Patchen. Chicago *Sun Book Week*, 7 November 1943.

Lawrence, D. H. *Studies in Classic American Literature*. New York: Thomas Seltzer, 1923.

Lazarus, H. P. Review of *Cloth of the Tempest*, by Kenneth Patchen. *The Nation* 158 (15 January 1944): 80.

Legge, James, trans. *The Texts of Taoism*. 2 vols. New York: Dover, 1962.

Le Maître, Georges. *From Cubism to Surrealism in French Literature*. Cambridge: Harvard University Press, 1941.

Leuba, James H. *The Psychology of Religious Mysticism*. New York: Harcourt Brace, 1925.

Levertov, Denise. "Some Notes on Organic Form." In *Naked Poetry*, edited by Stephen Berg and Robert Mezey, pp. 141–45. Indianapolis: Bobbs-Merrill, 1969.

Lozar, Tom. "*Before the Brave*: Portrait of Man as a Young Artist." In *Kenneth Patchen: A Collection of Essays*, edited by Richard Morgan, pp. 193–207. New York: AMS Press, 1977.

Maclear, J. F. " 'Heart of New England Rent': The Mystical Element in Early Puritan History." *Mississippi Valley Historical Review* 42 (1956): 621–52.

McGovern, Hugh. "Kenneth Patchen's Prose Works." *New Mexico Quarterly* 21 (1951): 189–97.

Merton, Thomas. *The Ascent to Truth*. New York: Harcourt Brace, 1951.

———. *The Sign of Jonas*. New York: Harcourt Brace, 1953.

Miller, Henry. *The Air-Conditioned Nightmare*. New York: New Directions, 1945.

———. *The Books in My Life*. New York: New Directions, 1952.

———. *The Colossus of Maroussi*. New York: New Directions, 1958.

———. *Patchen: Man of Anger and Light*. New York: Padell, 1947.

———. *Remember to Remember*. New York: New Directions, 1947.

———. *Stand Still Like the Hummingbird*. New York: New Directions, 1962.

———. *Tropic of Capricorn*. New York: Grove Press, 1961.

———. *The Wisdom of the Heart*. Norfolk, Conn.: New Directions, 1941.

Miller, James E., Jr. *A Critical Guide to Leaves of Grass*. Chicago: University of Chicago Press, 1966.

Miller, J. Hillis. *Poets of Reality*. Cambridge: Harvard University Press, 1965.

Miller, Perry. *Errand into the Wilderness*. Cambridge: Harvard University Press, 1956.

Moore, Peter. "Mystical Experience, Mystical Doctrine, Mystical Technique." In *Mysticism and Philosophical Analysis*, edited by Steven T. Katz, pp. 101–31. New York: Oxford University Press, 1978.

Morgan, Richard. "*The Journal of Albion Moonlight*: Its Form and Meaning." In *Kenneth Patchen: A Collection of Essays*, edited by Richard Morgan, pp. 152–80. New York: AMS Press, 1977.

Morris, Charles W. "Mysticism and Its Language." In *Language: An Enquiry into Its Meaning and Function*, edited by Ruth N. Anshen, pp. 179–87. New York: Harper and Brothers, 1957.

Mumford, Lewis. *The Conduct of Life*. New York: Harcourt Brace, 1951.

Nelson, Cary. *Our Last First Poets*. Urbana: University of Illinois Press, 1981.

Nelson, Raymond. "Mysticism and the Problems of Mystical Literature." *Rocky Mountain Review of Language and Literature* 30 (1976): 1–26.

———. *Van Wyck Brooks: A Writer's Life*. New York: Dutton, 1981.

Neumann, Eric. "Mystical Man." In *The Mystic Vision: Papers from the Eranos Yearbooks*, vol. 4, edited by Joseph Campbell, pp. 375–415. Bollingen Series 30. Princeton: Princeton University Press, 1968.

Organ, Troy. "The Language of Mysticism." *The Monist* 47 (1963): 417–43.

Patchen, Kenneth. *The Argument of Innocence: A Selection from the Arts of Kenneth Patchen*, text by Peter Veres. Oakland: Scrimshaw Press, 1976.

———. *An Astonished Eye Looks out of the Air*. Waldport, Oreg.: Untide Press, 1945.

———. *Because It Is*. New York: New Directions, 1960.

———. *Before the Brave*. New York: Random House, 1936.

———. "Blake" in *Job: Invented & Engraved by William Blake*. New York: United Book Guild, 1947.

———. "Bury Them in God." In *New Directions in Prose and Poetry*, no. 4, edited by James Laughlin, pp. 128–44. Norfolk, Conn.: New Directions, 1939.

———. *But Even So*. New York: New Directions, 1968.

———. *Cloth of the Tempest*. New York: Harper and Brothers, 1943.

———. *Collected Poems*. New York: New Directions, 1968.

———. *The Dark Kingdom*. New York: Harriss & Givens, 1942.

———. *Don't Look Now [Now You See It]*. In *Patchen's Lost Plays*, edited by Richard G. Morgan, pp. 13–67. Santa Barbara: Capra Press, 1977.

———. *Fables and Other Little Tales*. Karlsruhe/Baden: Jonathan Williams, 1953.

———. *The Famous Boating Party and Other Poems in Prose*. New York: New Directions, 1954.

———. *First Will & Testament*. Norfolk, Conn.: New Directions, 1939.

———. "from 'A Note on *The Hunted City*.' " In *Naked Poetry*, edited by Stephen Berg and Robert Mezey, p. 69. Indianapolis: Bobbs-Merrill, 1969.

———. *Hallelujah Anyway*. New York: New Directions, 1966.

———. *Hurrah for Anything*. Highlands, N.C.: Jonathan Williams, 1957.

———. *The Journal of Albion Moonlight*. Mount Vernon, N.Y.: privately printed, 1941.

———. *Love & War Poems, whisper & shout* 1 (special Patchen issue).

Derby, England: Whisper and Shout, 1968.

_____. *The Love Poems of Kenneth Patchen*. San Francisco: City Lights, 1960.

_____. *Memoirs of a Shy Pornographer*. New York: New Directions, 1945.

_____. "A Mercy-Filled & Defiant Xmas To All Still Worthy To Be Called Men." *Mano-Mano* 2 (1971): 63–64.

_____. *The Moment*. Alhambra, Calif.: privately printed, 1960.

_____. *Orchards, Thrones & Caravans*. N.p.: The Print Workshop, 1952.

_____. *Outlaw of the Lowest Planet*. Edited by David Gascoyne. London: Grey Walls Press, 1946.

_____. *Panels for the Walls of Heaven*. Berkeley, Calif.: Bern Porter, 1946.

_____. *Pictures of Life and of Death*. New York: Padell, 1946.

_____. *Poemscapes*. Highlands, N.C.: Jonathan Williams, 1957.

_____. *Red Wine & Yellow Hair*. New York: New Directions, 1949.

_____. *See You in the Morning*. New York: Padell, 1947.

_____. *Sleepers Awake*. New York: Padell, 1946.

_____. *The Teeth of the Lion*. Norfolk, Conn.: New Directions, 1942.

_____. *Tell You That I Love You*. Kansas City, Mo.: Hallmark, 1971.

_____. *There's Love All Day*. Kansas City, Mo.: Hallmark, 1970.

_____. *They Keep Riding Down All the Time*. New York: Padell, 1946.

_____. *To Say If You Love Someone*. Prairie City, Ill.: The Decker Press, 1948.

_____. *When We Were Here Together*. New York: New Directions, 1957.

_____. *Wonderings*. New York: New Directions, 1971.

Rauch, Frederick A. *Psychology: or, A View of the Human Soul*. New York: M. W. Dodd, 1840.

Reps, Paul. *Zen Flesh, Zen Bones*. Rutland, Vt.: C. E. Tuttle, 1957.

Rexroth, Kenneth. *Bird in the Bush*. New York: New Directions, 1958.

Royce, Josiah. *The World and the Individual*. New York: Dover, 1959.

Saint John of the Cross [Juan de Yepes]. *Complete Works*. Edited by E. Allison Peers. 3 vols. Westminister, Md.: Newman Bookshop, 1946.

Sanders, Jo. "Zen Buddhism and the Japanese Haiku." In *Anagogic Qualities of Literature*. Yearbook of Comparative Literature, vol. 4, edited by Joseph P. Strelka, pp. 211–17. University Park: Pennsylvania State University Press, 1971.

Scharfstein, Ben-ami. *Mystical Experience*. Oxford and Baltimore: Blackwell, 1973.

Schwartz, Delmore. " 'I Feel Drunk All the Time.' " *Nation* 164 (22 February 1947): 220, 222.

Smith, Larry R. *Kenneth Patchen*. Boston: Twayne, 1978.

Staal, Fritz. *Exploring Mysticism*. Berkeley: University of California Press, 1975.

Stace, W. T. *Mysticism and Philosophy*. Philadelphia and New York: Lippincott, 1960.

Steinbeck, John. *The Log from The Sea of Cortez*. New York: Viking, 1962.

Stevens, Wallace. "William Carlos Williams." In *William Carlos Williams*, edited by J. Hillis Miller, pp. 62–65. Englewood Cliffs, N.J.: Prentice-Hall, 1966.

Stovall, Floyd. *The Foreground of Leaves of Grass*. Charlottesville: University of Virginia Press, 1974.

Taylor, Frajam. "Puck in the Gardens of the Sun." *Poetry* 70 (1947): 269–74.

Trismosin, Solomon. *Splendor Solis*. London: Kegan Paul, Trench, Trubner and Company, n.d.

Trueblood, D. Elton. "The fullness of the Godhead dwelt in every blade of grass." In *The Quaker Reader*, edited by Jessamyn West, pp. 332–34. New York: Viking, 1962.

Underhill, Evelyn. *Mysticism*. New York: World, 1955.

Untermeyer, Jean Starr. "Problem of Patchen." *Saturday Review of Literature* 30 (22 March 1947): 15–16.

The Upanishads. Translated by Swami Prabhavananda and Frederick Manchester. New York: New American Library, 1957.

Walton, E. L. Review of *First Will & Testament*, by Kenneth Patchen. *New York Times Book Review*, 21 January 1940.

Warren, Robert Penn. Review of *The Dark Kingdom*, by Kenneth Patchen. *The Nation* 155 (4 July 1942): 220, 222.

Watts, Alan W. *The Spirit of Zen*. New York: Grove Press, 1960.

———. *The Way of Zen*. New York: New American Library, 1959.

Whitman, Walt. *Leaves of Grass: The First (1855) Edition*. Edited by Malcolm Cowley. New York: Viking, 1959.

———. *Leaves of Grass*. 3d edition. Boston: Thayer & Eldridge, 1860.

———. *Leaves of Grass*. Comprehensive Reader's Edition. Edited by Harold W. Blodgett and Sculley Bradley. New York: New York University Press, 1965.

———. *Prose Works 1892*. Edited by Floyd Stovall. 2 vols. New York: New York University Press, 1964.

Wilder, Amos N. *The Spiritual Aspects of the New Poetry*. New York:

Harper and Brothers, 1940.

Williams, William Carlos. "America, Whitman, and the Art of Poetry." *The Poetry Journal* 8 (November 1917): 27–36.

_____. *The Autobiography of William Carlos Williams.* New York: Random House, 1951.

_____. *The Collected Earlier Poems.* New York: New Directions, 1951.

_____. *In the American Grain.* New York: New Directions, 1956.

_____. Introduction to *Howl and Other Poems* by Allen Ginsberg. San Francisco: City Lights, 1956.

_____. *I Wanted to Write a Poem.* Edited by Edith Heal. Boston: Beacon Press, 1958.

_____. *Paterson.* New York: New Directions, 1963.

_____. *The Selected Letters of William Carlos Williams.* New York: McDowell Obolensky, 1957.

_____. *Spring and All.* In *Imaginations*, edited by Webster Schott, pp. 83–151. New York: New Directions, n.d.

Wilson, Edmund. *The Shores of Light.* New York: Farrar, Straus and Giroux, 1952.

Winters, Yvor. *In Defense of Reason.* Denver: Alan Swallow, 1947.

Zaehner, R. C. *Mysticism Sacred and Profane.* Oxford: Clarendon Press, 1957.

Index